DYNAMIC EARTH

Anthea Maton
Former NSTA National Coordinator
Project Scope, Sequence, Coordination
Washington, DC

Jean Hopkins
Science Instructor and Department Chairperson
John H. Wood Middle School
San Antonio, Texas

Susan Johnson
Professor of Biology
Ball State University
Muncie, Indiana

David LaHart
Senior Instructor
Florida Solar Energy Center
Cape Canaveral, Florida

Charles William McLaughlin
Science Instructor and Department Chairperson
Central High School
St. Joseph, Missouri

Maryanna Quon Warner
Science Instructor
Del Dios Middle School
Escondido, California

Jill D. Wright
Professor of Science Education
Director of International Field Programs
University of Pittsburgh
Pittsburgh, Pennsylvania

Prentice Hall
Englewood Cliffs, New Jersey
Needham, Massachusetts

Prentice Hall Science
Dynamic Earth

Student Text and Annotated Teacher's Edition
Laboratory Manual
Teacher's Resource Package
Teacher's Desk Reference
Computer Test Bank
Teaching Transparencies
Science Reader
Product Testing Activities
Computer Courseware
Video and Interactive Video

The illustration on the cover, rendered by Keith Kasnot, shows one of the most dynamic events on Earth—the eruption of a volcano.

Credits begin on page 177.

FIRST EDITION

ISBN 0-13-981119-2

4 5 6 7 8 9 10   96 95 94 93

Prentice Hall
A Division of Simon & Schuster
Englewood Cliffs, New Jersey 07632

STAFF CREDITS

Editorial:	Harry Bakalian, Pamela E. Hirschfeld, Maureen Grassi, Robert P. Letendre, Elisa Mui Eiger, Lorraine Smith-Phelan, Christine A. Caputo
Design:	AnnMarie Roselli, Carmela Pereira, Susan Walrath, Leslie Osher, Art Soares
Production:	Suse Cioffi, Joan McCulley, Elizabeth Torjussen, Christina Burghard, Marlys Lehmann
Photo Research:	Libby Forsyth, Emily Rose, Martha Conway
Publishing Technology:	Andrew Grey Bommarito, Gwendollynn Waldron, Deborah Jones, Monduane Harris, Michael Colucci, Gregory Myers, Cleasta Wilburn
Marketing:	Andy Socha, Victoria Willows
Pre-Press Production:	Laura Sanderson, Denise Herckenrath
Manufacturing:	Rhett Conklin, Gertrude Szyferblatt

Consultants

Kathy French	National Science Consultant
William Royalty	National Science Consultant

CONTENTS

DYNAMIC EARTH

Reference Section

Features

CONCEPT MAPPING

Throughout your study of science, you will learn a variety of terms, facts, figures, and concepts. Each new topic you encounter will provide its own collection of words and ideas—which, at times, you may think seem endless. But each of the ideas within a particular topic is related in some way to the others. No concept in science is isolated. Thus it will help you to understand the topic if you see the whole picture; that is, the interconnectedness of all the individual terms and ideas. This is a much more effective and satisfying way of learning than memorizing separate facts.

Actually, this should be a rather familiar process for you. Although you may not think about it in this way, you analyze many of the elements in your daily life by looking for relationships or connections. For example, when you look at a collection of flowers, you may divide them into groups: roses, carnations, and daisies. You may then associate colors with these flowers: red, pink, and white. The general topic is flowers. The subtopic is types of flowers. And the colors are specific terms that describe flowers. A topic makes more sense and is more easily understood if you understand how it is broken down into individual ideas and how these ideas are related to one another and to the entire topic.

It is often helpful to organize information visually so that you can see how it all fits together. One technique for describing related ideas is called a **concept map**. In a concept map, an idea is represented by a word or phrase enclosed in a box. There are several ideas in any concept map. A connection between two ideas is made with a line. A word or two that describes the connection is written on or near the line. The general topic is located at the top of the map. That topic is then broken down into subtopics, or more specific ideas, by branching lines. The most specific topics are located at the bottom of the map.

To construct a concept map, first identify the important ideas or key terms in the chapter or section. Do not try to include too much information. Use your judgment as to what is really important. Write the general topic at the top of your map. Let's use an example to help illustrate this process. Suppose you decide that the key terms in a section you are reading are School, Living Things, Language Arts, Subtraction, Grammar, Mathematics, Experiments, Papers, Science, Addition, Novels. The general topic is School. Write and enclose this word in a box at the top of your map.

SCHOOL

Now choose the subtopics—Language Arts, Science, Mathematics. Figure out how they are related to the topic. Add these words to your map. Continue this procedure until you have included all the important ideas and terms. Then use lines to make the appropriate connections between ideas and terms. Don't forget to write a word or two on or near the connecting line to describe the nature of the connection.

Do not be concerned if you have to redraw your map (perhaps several times!) before you show all the important connections clearly. If, for example, you write papers for Science as well as for Language Arts, you may want to place these two subjects next to each other so that the lines do not overlap.

One more thing you should know about concept mapping: Concepts can be correctly mapped in many different ways. In fact, it is unlikely that any two people will draw identical concept maps for a complex topic. Thus there is no one correct concept map for any topic! Even

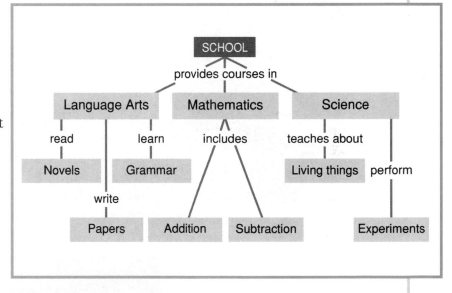

though your concept map may not match those of your classmates, it will be correct as long as it shows the most important concepts and the clear relationships among them. Your concept map will also be correct if it has meaning to you and if it helps you understand the material you are reading. A concept map should be so clear that if some of the terms are erased, the missing terms could easily be filled in by following the logic of the concept map.

DYNAMIC EARTH

▲ Waterfalls and streams slowly wear away the rock of the island's interior.

Lava spews forth from the top of Mauna Loa and flows in orange rivers down its slopes. ▶

It is midnight on the island of Hawaii. The stars shine brightly in a coal-black sky; they look close enough to touch. But in one part of the sky above a distant mountain ridge, something strange is happening.

Red and purple clouds swirl rapidly and restlessly, rumbling with thunder. Just below them, there is an eerie reddish glow. Orange and yellow flames flicker along the ridge, forming a shimmering curtain of fire.

Through your binoculars, you can see that this is no ordinary fire. Fountains of molten rock the colors of flame leap from cracks in the Earth and fall back to the ground in showers of black cinders. Scarlet streams of molten rock ooze from the cracks and flow away, creating twisted formations of black rock as they cool.

Even as the island is being built up in one place, it is being broken down in another. Waves pound against the island's shore, grinding the rocks of the coast into sand and carrying the sand away. Farther inland, rocks are broken down into soil by wind, rain, and plants. Like the rest of the dynamic Earth, the island is constantly changing.

Waves crash along the shore, breaking down rock born of volcanic activity.

Discovery *Activity*

Sand

1. Examine some sand with a magnifying glass. What do you observe?

2. Form a pile of sand in a large waterproof container such as a dishpan. Pour water from a paper cup onto the sand. Does the speed at which you pour make a difference in what you observe?

3. Fill the bottom of a small plastic container to a depth of 2 centimeters with wet sand. Stir 25 grams of alum into the sand. Allow the mixture to dry completely (about 2 days). After the mixture has dried, gently twist the sides of the container to free its contents.

    ■ How do you think the observations you made in this activity relate to events that occur in nature?

Movement of the Earth's Crust

Have you ever had the exhilarating experience of standing at the edge of a mountain and looking down into a valley far below? Did you know that millions of years ago the mountain and valley probably looked quite different? The land may have been completely flat, without so much as a hill. Perhaps the area was once beneath an ocean. What caused the land to change? How did the mountain and the valley form?

Throughout the Earth's long history, its surface has been lifted up, pushed down, bent, and broken by forces beneath the surface. Although the resulting movements of the Earth's surface are usually too small and too slow to be directly observed, they are constantly changing the appearance of the Earth. Thus the Earth looks different today from the way it did millions of years ago. For example, what were once small hills may now be mountains that stand almost 9 kilometers above sea level!

What are the forces that cause mountains and valleys to form and grow? How do they work? Read on and find out.

Journal *Activity*

You and Your World   Perhaps you have hiked to the top of a high mountain, traveled down into a valley, or imagined doing so. In your journal, discuss your experiences, real or imagined. Accompany your description with some illustrations.

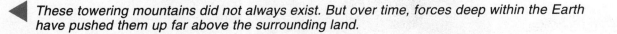

These towering mountains did not always exist. But over time, forces deep within the Earth have pushed them up far above the surrounding land.

Guide for Reading

*Focus on these questions as
you read.*

▶ How does the formation of
mountains, valleys,
plateaus, and domes relate
to stress?

▶ How do faulting and folding
change the appearance of
the Earth's surface?

1–1 Earth's Changing Surface

Stress! This word is probably all too familiar to most people. Think about the last time you were under a lot of stress. Perhaps you were getting ready to take a hard math test, arguing with a friend or family member, making a difficult decision, or waiting for your turn to perform in a musical or athletic competition. You may have felt as if you were being pulled in many directions at once. Or you may have felt so tense inside that you thought something might snap.

Like you, the Earth also experiences **stress**. This kind of stress, however, is not the result of emotionally difficult situations. Rather, it is caused by forces within the Earth itself. These forces push and pull on the part of the Earth known as the **crust**. The crust is the surface, or outermost, layer of the Earth.

There are two major sections of the crust. One section is called continental crust. Continental crust makes up the Earth's landmasses, such as the North American continent. In most places, continental crust is about 32 kilometers thick. But under tall mountains, it can be up to 70 kilometers thick.

The other section of the crust is called oceanic crust. Oceanic crust is found under the ocean floor. It is thinner than continental crust. Oceanic crust is usually about 8 kilometers thick.

Figure 1–1 *The rocks of
the Earth's crust may be
carved into strange and
beautiful forms by the
action of wind, water, and
weather. The Needle's
Eye is found in the Black
Hills of South Dakota
(left). The red–orange
pinnacles are found in
Bryce Canyon National
Park in Utah (right).*

Figure 1–2 *These rocks on the coast of New Zealand have been deformed by stress. What does the term deformation mean?*

As you have just read, stress pushes and pulls on the Earth's crust. **As the rocks of the crust undergo stress, they slowly change shape and volume.** (Volume is the amount of space an object takes up.) **They also move up or down or sideways.** The movement causes the rocks to break, tilt, and fold. The breaking, tilting, and folding of rocks is called **deformation.** The prefix *de-* means undo; the root word *form* means shape or configuration. Can you explain why the term deformation is appropriate?

There are three basic types of stress, each of which deforms the crust in a different way. The three types of stress are **compression, tension,** and **shearing.** Refer to Figure 1–3 as you read about these different types of stress.

Compression squeezes the rocks of the crust. This often causes the particles in the crustal rocks to

Figure 1–3 *Each of the different forms of stress deforms the crust in a different way. The large arrows show the directions in which the forms of stress push or pull at rocks. How are rocks affected by compression? Tension? Shearing?*

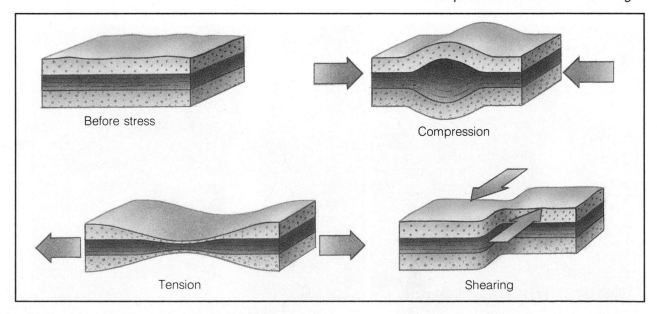

Before stress

Compression

Tension

Shearing

The Changing Earth

1. During the next two months, collect newspaper clippings dealing with earthquakes, floods, volcanoes, and other Earth-changing events.

2. On a map of the world, indicate the site of each event. Use a different-colored pencil for each category of event. Include a key with your map.

■ How did each event alter the Earth's surface?

move closer together, making the rocks denser and smaller in volume. In this case, compression is acting rather like a trash compactor, squeezing a large amount of matter into a smaller amount of space. As crustal rocks are compressed, they are pushed both higher up and deeper down. To understand this movement, imagine you are squeezing clay in your hand. As you squeeze the clay, some of it is pushed out of the opening at the top of your fist and some of it is pushed out of the opening at the bottom.

Tension pulls on the rocks of the crust, causing them to stretch out over a larger area. Like a piece of warm taffy being pulled, a rock under tension becomes thinner in the middle than at the ends. In addition, as the volume of the rock increases, its density decreases.

Shearing pushes rocks of the crust in two opposite directions. This causes the rocks to twist or tear apart. During shearing, then, rocks are not compressed or stretched. They simply bend or break apart.

Compression, tension, and shearing can change a rock's volume, its shape, or both. These stresses can also cause the rocks to **fracture,** or crack. If the rocks fracture along numerous flat surfaces which show no displacement, the cracks are called joints. Joints are generally parallel to one another. Some rocks have joints that form in more than one direction. Such rocks may break into blocks. The blocks form where the different sets of joints cross one another.

Figure 1–4 *Joints divide the face of the cliff behind the waterfall into tall, six-sided blocks. The joints formed as molten rock cooled and shrank. What shape are the blocks formed by the joints in the cliff overlooking the sea?*

Figure 1–5 *Based on the diagram and the photograph, what type of stress was acting on the sandstone? How can you tell?*

Faulting

Stress sometimes causes rocks to break. A break or crack along which rocks move is called a **fault.** The rocks on one side of the fault slide past the rocks on the other side of the fault. Movements along a fault can be up, down, or sideways. Earthquakes often occur along faults in the Earth's crust. What are some other possible results of movements along a fault?

Look at the cross sections of faulted rocks in Figure 1–5. As you can see, there are two blocks of rock, one on top of the other. The block of rock above the fault is called the **hanging wall.** The block below the fault is called the **foot wall.**

Stress can cause either the hanging wall or the foot wall to move up or down along a fault. If tension is acting on a fault, the hanging wall will move down relative to the foot wall. If this occurs, the fault between the two blocks is called a **normal fault.** If compression is acting on a fault, the hanging wall will move up relative to the foot wall. This type of fault is called a **reverse fault.**

A special type of reverse fault is a **thrust fault.** A thrust fault is formed when compression causes the hanging wall to slide over the foot wall. Thrust faults are special because they are almost horizontal, whereas regular reverse faults and normal faults are almost vertical. Thrust faults usually carry rocks many kilometers from their original position. Rocks are usually severely bent at the same time that thrust faulting occurs. In addition, thrust faults mix up the order of the layers in rock. Normally, older rock layers are found under younger rock layers. But a thrust fault pushes older rocks on top of younger rocks. The Lewis Overthrust Fault in Glacier National Park, Montana, is an example of a thrust fault. Here very old rocks have slid eastward more than 48 kilometers and now rest on top of younger rocks.

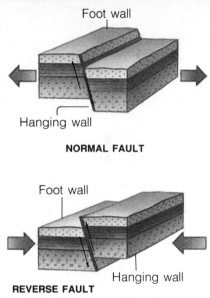

Figure 1–6 *A thrust fault is a special kind of reverse fault in which the foot wall slides over the hanging wall. How does a thrust fault affect the order of the rock layers in an area?*

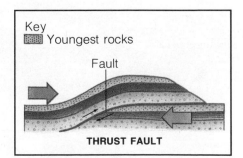

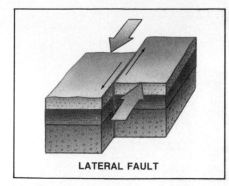

LATERAL FAULT

Figure 1–7 *In a lateral fault, which is also known as a strike-slip fault, the blocks of rock move horizontally past each other.*

Stress does not cause blocks of crustal rock to move only up and down. Shearing will cause the blocks of rock to slide horizontally past each other. One block moves to the left or right in relation to the other block. The fault along which the blocks move horizontally past each other is called a **lateral fault.**

Faulted Mountains and Valleys

When there are many normal faults in one area, a series of mountains and valleys may form. Mountains formed by blocks of rock uplifted by normal faults are called **fault-block mountains.** A vast region in western North America called the Cordilleran Mountain region contains many fault-block mountains. The region extends from central Mexico to Oregon and Idaho and includes western Utah, all of Nevada, and eastern California.

Valleys also form when mountains form. Some valleys are formed when the block of land between two normal faults slides downward. Valleys created in this way are called **rift valleys.** One example of a rift valley is Death Valley in California. It is a long, narrow valley 87 meters below sea level. Scientists believe that the valley was formed by a series of small movements along two faults at either side of the valley. They estimate that the land along the eastern fault of Death Valley will move another 3 meters during the next 1000 years.

Figure 1–8 *A fault-block mountain is formed when a block (or blocks) of rocks between two normal faults is pushed up. The rock layers in the diagram are flat, so you can clearly see the mountain-forming process. However, the rock layers in real mountains, such as the Grand Tetons in Wyoming, are usually tilted. One of the slopes of each mountain was once a horizontal surface!*

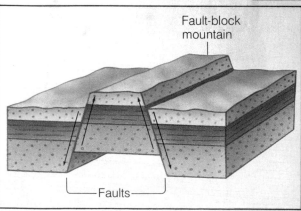

Fault-block mountain

Faults

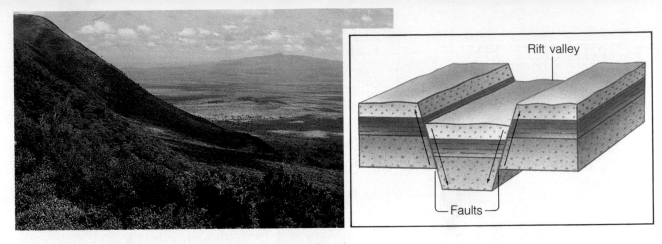

Figure 1–9 *A rift valley is formed when a block of rock between two normal faults slides down. The flat plain formed by this Kenyan rift valley is home to zebras, wildebeest, lions, and many other living things. How did the low mountains on either side of the valley form?*

Folding

Sometimes when stress is applied to the rocks of the crust, the rocks bend but do not break. The rocks bend in much the same way a rug wrinkles as it is pushed across a floor. A bend in a rock is called a **fold.** As you can see in Figure 1–10, a rock can fold either upward or downward. An upward fold in a rock is called an **anticline** (AN-tih-klighn). A downward fold in a rock is called a **syncline** (SIHN-klighn).

Folds vary in size. Some folds are so small that you need a magnifying glass to see them clearly. Others are large enough to form mountains. Layered rocks with large folds often have smaller folds within the layers. The Appalachian Mountains in the eastern United States are made up of many anticlines and synclines. This folded mountain chain extends from Canada to Alabama.

Figure 1–10 *Anticlines are upward folds in rocks. Synclines are downward folds in rocks. Some folds are quite large. The speck at the top of the English hill is a person.*

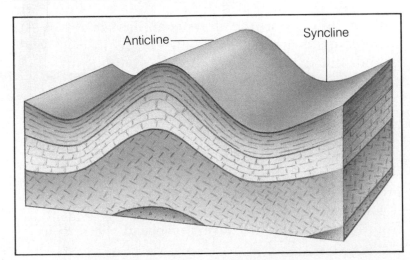

Under Pressure

1. Flatten three pieces of different-colored modeling clay into thin, rectangular layers on a piece of waxed paper. (If you do not have clay, you can substitute three equal-sized carpet scraps or pieces of foam rubber.)

2. Place the flattened layers of clay on top of one another.

3. Place your hands at opposite ends of the clay rectangle. Slowly push the two ends together. What happens to the clay?

■ How does this relate to the processes that build mountains?

Even though an anticline is an upward fold, it is not always higher than the surrounding land. An anticline can be under hills, valleys, or flat areas. An anticline may be hidden by layers of rock that build up in the low-lying areas around it after it forms. Or the stress may not have been great enough to bring the fold to the Earth's surface.

Fault or Fold?

A number of factors determine whether rocks will fault or fold. One factor is temperature. If the rocks become extremely hot during compression, they are more likely to fold than to fault. Do you know why? If you ever left a box of crayons in the sun when you were young, you may have firsthand experience with the effect of temperature on folding and faulting. At normal temperatures, crayons snap in two when stress is applied. In other words, they fault. But warm crayons can bend without breaking—they fold.

Another factor that affects whether rocks will fault or fold is pressure. The greater the pressure applied to the rocks, the more likely they are to fold rather than fault.

Rock type is yet another factor that determines whether rocks will fault or fold. Some types of rocks break easily when stress is applied. Such fragile rocks are said to be brittle. Sandstone is one example of brittle rock. Other rocks, such as rock salt, bend easily under stress. Rocks that bend easily are said to be ductile. Ductile rocks are more likely to fold, whereas brittle rocks are more likely to fault.

Another factor that determines whether rocks will fault or fold is how the stress is applied to the rocks. If the stress is applied gradually, the rocks will usually fold. But if the stress is applied suddenly, the rocks will usually fault.

Plateaus

A **plateau** (pla-TOH) is a large area of flat land that is raised high above sea level. You can get a pretty good idea of what a typical plateau looks like if you place a sandwich on a plate and look at it from the side. The flat layers of bread slices, cold cuts, cheese, lettuce, tomato, and mayonnaise (or whatever you put in your sandwich) correspond roughly to the horizontal rock layers that make up a plateau. Like a sandwich, a plateau is wider than it is tall. In addition, a plateau is often surrounded by steep cliffs that rise sharply from the surrounding land, much as a sandwich rises above the surface of the plate on which it is placed.

Although plateaus are often raised up by the same processes that form mountains, the rock layers in a plateau remain flat. (This is not the case with mountains, in which the rock layers are tilted and broken by faulting or are warped by folding.)

One way a plateau may be formed is by a slow, flat-topped fold. The Appalachian Plateau, which lies just west of the folded Appalachian Mountains, was created millions of years ago by such a fold. This plateau covers much of New York, Pennsylvania, Ohio, Kentucky, West Virginia, and Tennessee.

Another way a plateau may be formed is through vertical faulting. The Colorado Plateau, which is located west of the Rocky Mountains, was uplifted when the underlying region of the inner Earth became hotter and expanded. As this region expanded, it pushed up on the crust above it. The rocks at the edge of the forming Colorado Plateau fractured, and the plateau was slowly pushed upward. The Colorado Plateau covers parts of New Mexico, western

Figure 1–11 *A river cutting through the Colorado plateau reveals the horizontal rock layers that lie beneath its surface (left). Lake Titicaca is located on a plateau on the border of Peru and Bolivia. Rock, mud, and sand washed down from the sides of the surrounding mountains and piled up in flat layers to form the plateau (right). How else are plateaus formed?*

Colorado, eastern Utah, and northern Arizona. Most of the plateau is more than 1500 meters above sea level. The Colorado Plateau was formed hundreds of millions of years after the Appalachian Plateau.

Plateaus can also be formed by a series of molten rock flows on the surface of the Earth. Molten rock at the surface of the Earth is called lava. Molten rock deep within the Earth is called magma. Magma reaches the Earth's surface through long cracks in the ground. Great floods of hot molten rock periodically stream out of the cracks. The flowing lava spreads out over a large area and hardens into a sheet. The lava sometimes fills in valleys and covers hills. The flowing and spreading out of the lava is repeated over and over again. The hardened lava sheets pile up and form a raised plateau. The Columbia Plateau, which covers parts of Oregon, Washington, and Idaho, is a lava plateau. Here lava built up a large flat region covering almost 5 million square kilometers. The plateau is 1 to 2 kilometers thick.

Rivers often carve one large plateau into many smaller plateaus or cut deep valleys and canyons through plateaus. One of the most spectacular canyons formed by a river is the Grand Canyon in the Colorado Plateau.

Domes

You know now that lava flows out onto the Earth's surface to form plateaus. Sometimes, however, magma pushes upward but does not reach the Earth's surface. The stress caused by the magma causes the rock layers above it to fold upward, forming an uplifted area. At some point, the magma cools and forms hardened rock.

The uplifted area created by rising magma is called a **dome.** A dome is a raised area shaped roughly like the top half of a sphere. The outline of a dome is oval or circular. You can think of a dome as rather like a blister on the surface of the Earth. Like a blister, a dome is formed when fluid collects beneath the surface and pushes up on overlying layers, forming a raised spot in the immediate area but leaving the surrounding regions flat and undisturbed.

Figure 1–12 *A dome may be formed when rising magma causes the rock layers above it to fold upward (left). Over a long period of time, the uppermost rock layers may be worn away to reveal the dome's core of hardened magma (right).*

Dome

Magma

Domes that have been worn away in places form many separate peaks called dome mountains. The Black Hills of South Dakota and Wyoming are dome mountains. In this region, many layers of flat-lying rocks were arched up. Over a long period of time, the rocks on top were worn away. The hardened magma that caused the uplifting was then exposed.

1–1 Section Review

1. How does stress affect the Earth's crust?
2. Compare faulting and folding.
3. How are plateaus formed?
4. What is a dome? A dome mountain?

Connection—*Paleontology*

5. A paleontologist is a scientist who studies organisms that lived on the Earth long ago (such as dinosaurs). Most of the information about these long-gone organisms comes from fossils, or the preserved remains of ancient organisms. The majority of fossils are found in certain kinds of rock layers. Why is it important for a paleontologist to understand faulting and folding?

FIND OUT BY
WRITING

A Geological Trip

Using information from the text, write a 300-word essay about an imaginary trip you are taking across the United States. Describe any important and dramatic geological formations you find along the way. In your essay, use the following vocabulary words.

plateau
dome mountain
fault
anticline
thrust fault
fault-block mountain
rift valley
fold
syncline
normal fault

PROBLEM Solving

Studying Sidewalks

Ever since her class had started studying the movements of the Earth's crust in science, Jenny had noticed that she was paying a lot more attention to the ground at her feet. For example, she had observed that the sidewalk in her neighborhood had a number of cracks, sunken areas, raised bumps, seams, and breaks in it. In one place, one broken edge of the sidewalk stuck up two to three centimeters above the matching edge. As Jenny's brother had found out the hard way, it was easy to stub one's toe on that protruding edge.

Obviously, Jenny thought, the sidewalk was not made with cracks in it, or with low places where puddles formed, or with raised areas that tripped people. Like the Earth's crust, the sidewalk had changed. But why did it change?

Applying Concepts

1. What do you think causes the cracks and other changes in the sidewalk?

2. How are the forces that act on the sidewalk similar to the ones that act on the crust of the Earth? How are they different?

3. Suppose that Jenny hypothesizes that tree roots, acting rather like the magma in a dome, are responsible for a broken, raised ridge on the sidewalk. How might she test her hypothesis?

1–2 The Floating Crust

You have learned how areas of the Earth's crust can be moved up and down through faulting, folding, and uplifting. But there is another process in which the crust moves up and down. Here is how it works.

Beneath the Earth's crust is a layer called the **mantle.** The mantle is the layer of the Earth that

Figure 1–13 *These four diagrams show the effect a heavy icecap has on an area's elevation. When an icecap forms on a flat area of crust (A), the added material increases the force with which the area pushes down on the mantle. This causes the area to sink (B). When the icecap melts, the downward force of the crust decreases, so the upward force of the mantle pushes the crust slowly upward (C). Eventually, the upward force of the mantle balances the downward force of the crust (D). What is the balancing of these two forces called?*

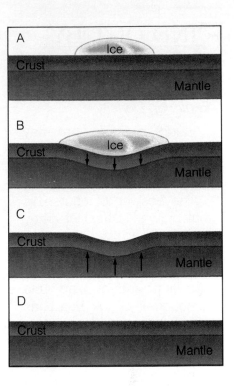

extends from the bottom of the crust downward about 2900 kilometers to the Earth's core. The mantle is made of rock that flows slowly—sort of like molasses or hot, thick tar. Because the mantle is much denser than the crust, the solid, rocky crust floats on the mantle. (A less dense object always floats on a more dense object.)

The floating crust exerts a downward force on the mantle. But the mantle also exerts a force. The mantle exerts an upward force on the crust. **A balance exists between the downward force of the crust and the upward force of the mantle.** The balancing of these two forces is called **isostasy** (igh-SAHS-tuh-see). The prefix *iso-* means equal, and the root word

Figure 1–14 *Material carried by rivers is deposited on the ocean floor, where it builds up in thick, heavy layers. You might think that eventually the ocean would be filled in. But this does not happen. Why?*

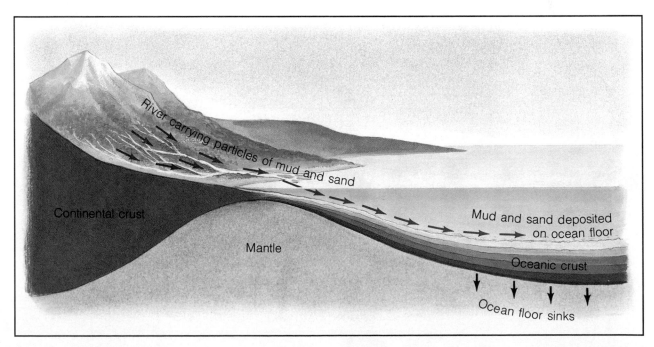

FIND OUT BY DOING

Exploring Density

Here's a riddle that may be familiar to you: Which is heavier—a pound of feathers or a pound of lead?

The answer, of course, is that neither is heavier. They weigh exactly the same amount. However, a pound of feathers fills a large bag and a pound of lead is a rather small chunk. Lead has more mass per unit volume than feathers do. In other words, lead has a greater density.

How do the densities of other substances compare to one another? Find out for yourself. Some materials that you might use in your experiments include a large glass jar, water, vegetable oil, glycerine, food coloring, ice, salt, a block of wood, a small plastic object, and a rock.

■ Which substances have the greatest density? The least density? How can you tell?

■ How might density account for the fact that mountains are high and oceans are deep?

stasis means standing still. Why is isostasy an appropriate term for this balancing act?

If material is added to an area of the crust, that area will float lower on the mantle. If material is removed, that area will float higher. So the crust is always balanced on the mantle.

Isostasy explains why some low-lying regions—such as Norway, Sweden, and Finland—have slowly risen. Thousands of years ago, these northern European countries were covered by tons of ice. The melting of the ice removed material from the crust. As a result, the land began to float higher on the mantle. In fact, the land is still rising today—and it is expected to rise about 200 meters in the next few thousand years! What do you think would happen to the elevation of Antarctica if the ice sheets covering most of the continent melted?

Crustal rock can also sink. For example, the Mississippi River has dropped millions of tons of mud and sand particles into the Gulf of Mexico. Will the accumulation of particles cause the Gulf to grow shallower and eventually disappear? Thanks to isostasy, the answer is no. The addition of materials—mud and sand—to the crust on the Gulf floor causes it to sink. But the depth of the water in the Gulf has not changed. A balance is maintained between the building up and the sinking of the Gulf floor.

1-2 Section Review

1. What balances the downward force of the crust? What is this balancing of forces called?
2. Which are less dense, the crustal rocks or the mantle rocks?
3. What happens when sediments are deposited on the ocean floor?

Critical Thinking—*Applying Concepts*

4. Most of Greenland is hidden beneath an enormous sheet of ice. Using what you have learned about isostasy, explain why the surface rock that makes up Greenland is saucer-shaped, with its center below sea level.

CONNECTIONS

A World of Opposites

According to traditional Chinese *philosophy*, everything that exists is made up of two opposite principles: the feminine *yin* and the masculine *yang*. These two principles interact and balance each other; when one increases, the other decreases. The harmonizing of these two opposite principles is represented by a circle divided into light and dark halves.

Consider what you have learned about the movement of the Earth's crust. You have learned about tension and compression, anticlines and synclines, and the balancing of upward and downward forces in isostasy. What other opposites can you think of?

Geology (the study of the Earth) is not the only science in which you will find opposites. In chemistry, there are positive and negative ions, acids and bases, metallic and nonmetallic elements.

In biology, there are seed plants and plants without seeds, males and females, vertebrate and invertebrate animals. In physics, there are concave and convex lenses, north and south magnetic poles, positive and negative electrodes. The world of opposites is not restricted to the world of science. There are representational and abstract works of art. Music may be fortissimo (very loud) or pianissimo (very soft). Numbers may be even or odd, real or imaginary, rational or irrational, positive or negative. Dramas may be tragedies or comedies and may receive favorable or unfavorable reviews. Religions deal with good and evil. The law deals with right and wrong. What other pairs of opposites can you think of?

Laboratory Investigation

Examining Isostasy

Problem

How does the Earth's crust float on the Earth's mantle?

Materials (per group)

2 blocks of wood—
    1: 10 cm x 10 cm x 2.5 cm
    2: 10 cm x 10 cm x 1.5 cm
basin of water
metric ruler
25 metal washers

	Number of Washers	Amount Above Water
Block 1		
Block 2		

Procedure

1. Label the larger block of wood 1 and the smaller block 2.

2. Float block 1 in the basin of water. Using a metric ruler, measure the amount of wood above the water's surface. Record your measurement in a data table similar to the one shown here.

3. Carefully place ten washers on the surface of block 1. Measure the amount of wood above the water's surface. Record this information in your data table.

4. Continue adding washers two at a time. Carefully measure and record the amount of wood above the water's surface after each addition. Stop adding washers when the wood sinks or the washers spill into the basin of water.

5. Repeat steps 2 through 4 for block 2.

Observations

1. Are there any differences in the way the two blocks of wood float before the washers are added? After?

2. Which block of wood is able to hold more washers before it sinks? Explain.

Analysis and Conclusions

1. How do the two blocks of wood resemble continental and oceanic crust? How does the water represent the Earth's mantle?

2. If block 1 represents continental crust and block 2 represents oceanic crust, which crust is able to support the most weight?

3. How is the Earth's crust able to stay balanced on the mantle?

4. How does this investigation illustrate isostasy?

5. **On Your Own** Design an experiment to examine isostasy in which thick mud is used to model the mantle. What do you think would be the results of this experiment? If you receive permission, you may perform this investigation and see if your predictions were correct.

Summarizing Key Concepts

1–1 Earth's Changing Surface

▲ As the rocks of the crust undergo stress, they slowly change shape and volume.

▲ The breaking, tilting, and folding of rocks is called deformation.

▲ Compression squeezes the rocks of the crust together.

▲ Tension pulls the rocks of the crust apart.

▲ Shearing pushes two parts of the crust in opposite directions, causing the rocks of the crust to twist or tear apart.

▲ A break or crack along which rocks move is called a fault. A break along which rocks do not move is a joint.

▲ The block of rock above a fault is called the hanging wall, and the block of rock below a fault is called the foot wall.

▲ Mountains formed by blocks of rock uplifted by normal faults are called fault-block mountains.

▲ Valleys formed when the block of land between two normal faults slides downward are called rift valleys.

▲ A bend in a rock is a fold. An upward fold is an anticline; a downward fold is a syncline.

▲ Rocks are more likely to fold than fault if they are hot, under pressure, ductile, and stressed gradually.

▲ A plateau is a large area of flat land that is raised high above sea level.

▲ Plateaus may be formed by flat-topped folds, vertical faulting, or lava flows.

▲ An uplifted area called a dome can be formed by magma that works its way toward the Earth's surface without actually erupting onto the surface and causes the rock layers above it to fold upward.

▲ Domes that have been worn away in places form many separate peaks, or dome mountains.

1–2 The Floating Crust

▲ The mantle is the layer of the Earth that extends from the core to the crust.

▲ The balancing of the downward force of the crust and the upward force of the mantle is known as isostasy.

Reviewing Key Terms

Define each term in a complete sentence.

1–1 Earth's Changing Surface

stress
crust
deformation
compression
tension
shearing
fracture
fault
hanging wall
foot wall

normal fault
reverse fault
thrust fault
lateral fault
fault-block mountain
rift valley
fold
anticline
syncline
plateau
dome

1–2 The Floating Crust

mantle
isostasy

Chapter Review

Content Review

Multiple Choice

Choose the letter of the answer that best completes each statement.

1. The rocky outermost layer of the Earth is the
   a. core.
   c. mantle.
   b. crust.
   d. continental plate.
2. The form of stress that pulls apart rocks of the crust is
   a. tension.
   c. contraction.
   b. compression.
   d. compaction.
3. The block of rock above a fault is called the
   a. anticline.
   c. foot wall.
   b. syncline.
   d. hanging wall.
4. Older rock layers may slide up and over younger rock layers in a
   a. normal fault.
   c. thrust fault.
   b. lateral fault.
   d. anticline.
5. Rocks are more likely to fault than fold if they are
   a. ductile.
   c. under much pressure.
   b. extremely hot.
   d. brittle.

6. A downward fold in a rock is called a(an)
   a. syncline.
   c. plateau.
   b. anticline.
   d. dome.
7. A large flat area that is uplifted high above sea level and whose underlying layers of rock are flat is called a(an)
   a. plateau.
   c. dome.
   b. syncline.
   d. anticline.
8. Magma pushing on rock layers may cause them to fold sharply upward into a blisterlike structure called a
   a. syncline.
   c. fault-block mountain.
   b. dome.
   d. plateau.
9. Which of the following is formed when the block of land between two normal faults slides downward?
   a. rift valley
   c. syncline
   b. anticline
   d. horst

True or False

If the statement is true, write "true." If it is false, change the underlined word or words to make the statement true.

1. The breaking, tilting, and folding of rock is called <u>shearing</u>.
2. The blocks of rock move horizontally past one another in a <u>normal fault</u>.
3. The balancing of the force exerted by the crust and the force exerted by the mantle is called <u>isostasy</u>.
4. <u>Brittle</u> rocks are more likely to fold than fault.
5. <u>Fault-block mountains</u> are formed by blocks of rock uplifted by normal faults.
6. A downward, U-shaped fold in the rocks is known as a(an) <u>dome</u>.
7. When <u>shearing</u> acts on a fault, the foot wall slides up relative to the hanging wall.

Concept Mapping

Complete the following concept map for Section 1–1. Refer to pages J6–J7 to construct a concept map for the entire chapter.

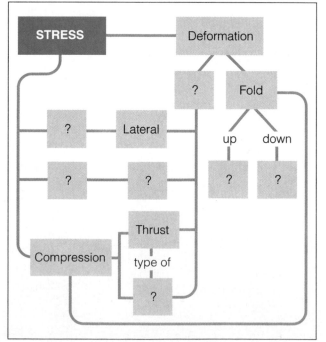

Concept Mastery

Discuss each of the following in a brief paragraph.

1. How can lava form a plateau?
2. What is the difference between a joint and a fault?
3. Compare magma and lava.
4. What is isostasy? How does isostasy affect the Earth's crust?
5. Draw a diagram that compares an anticline with a syncline.
6. How do faulting and folding result in deformation of the rocks of the crust?
7. How are compression, tension, and shearing similar? How are they different?

Critical Thinking and Problem Solving

Use the skills you have developed in this chapter to answer each of the following.

1. **Summarizing information** Prepare a table that summarizes what you have learned about the different kinds of faults. Your table should include the following information: type of fault; position of blocks; type of stress involved; sketch of fault.
2. **Making comparisons** Compare the rising and sinking of a floating ship to the floating crust.
3. **Relating concepts** Explain why a dome can be classified as an anticline. How does a dome differ from a more typical anticline?
4. **Interpreting data** Explain how the rock formation in the accompanying photograph was formed.

5. **Applying concepts** Geologists studying a rock formation have found that there are older rocks lying on top of younger rocks. How can you explain these findings in terms of faulting? In terms of folding? (*Hint:* Folds are not always symmetrical, or even on both sides.)
6. **Making inferences** Coal miners dig their tunnels along faults. The miners named the blocks above and below the faults. They called one block the hanging wall and the other block the foot wall. How do you think they came up with these names?
7. **Making generalizations** Rock salt is much less dense than surrounding rocks are. Under pressure, such as that caused by the weight of rock layers above it and around it, rock salt flows easily. Explain why and how rock salt, like magma, is able to form domes.
8. **Using the writing process** Imagine that you are an area of the Earth's crust. Write a brief autobiography describing the many changes due to stress that you have experienced over the millions of years of your existence. (*Hints:* What type of rock formation are you now? What were you in your "childhood"? Were the changes you experienced fun, scary, or exciting? How did they make you feel?)

Earthquakes and Volcanoes

Guide for Reading

After you read the following sections, you will be able to

2–1 Earthquakes

- Explain what happens during an earthquake.
- Describe how earthquakes are detected.

2–2 Formation of a Volcano

- Compare the different types of lava and volcanic particles.
- Classify the three types of volcanoes.

2–3 Volcano and Earthquake Zones

- Identify the locations of major zones of earthquake and volcanic activity.

It was the World Series. People filled Candlestick Park in San Francisco to watch the Giants play the Oakland Athletics. But the game scheduled for October 17, 1989, was not to be played. The blimp, floating high above the stadium, was strategically positioned to capture the drama of the game. But instead, the blimp was dispatched to film another drama—the drama of buildings cracking and fires breaking out as underground gas mains exploded. Sportscasters became newscasters as the focus of the baseball championship changed dramatically to the streets of San Francisco. If you tuned in to watch this World Series game, you saw a major earthquake "live."

It was July 1991, and huge black clouds of smoke poured from a volcano in the Philippines. During the eruption, molten rocks, poisonous fumes, and dust-laden air poured from Mount Pinatubo. The toll in lives and property damage mounted as the volcano continued to erupt.

Volcanoes and earthquakes are dramatic examples—and not so gentle reminders—that the Earth's crust is continually moving. In this chapter, you will learn what causes some movements of the Earth's crust and how these movements are studied. You will also learn about two of the most sudden and violent movements: earthquakes and volcanic eruptions.

Journal *Activity*

You and Your World Have you ever experienced an earthquake or seen a volcano erupt? What do you think it would be like to live through an earthquake or the eruption of a volcano? Write your thoughts in your journal.

During the October 1989 earthquake, buildings in many sections of San Francisco suddenly collapsed.

Guide for Reading

Focus on these questions as you read.
▶ *What is an earthquake?*
▶ *How does a seismograph work?*

2–1 Earthquakes

The Earth seems so solid—its surface strong and stable. But the occurrence of enormous natural disturbances such as earthquakes and volcanoes indicates that perceptions about the Earth's stability often differ from reality. The surface of the Earth actually moves in ways most dramatic. One has only to see the effects of an **earthquake** to appreciate this fact.

An earthquake is the shaking and trembling that results from the sudden movement of part of the Earth's crust. A familiar example will help you to understand how an earthquake behaves. When you throw a pebble into a pond, waves move outward in all directions. In a similar manner, when rocks in the Earth's crust break, earthquake waves travel through the Earth in all directions. The ground shakes and trembles. During a severe earthquake, the ground can rise and fall like waves in an ocean. The motion of the ground causes buildings, trees, and telephone poles to sway and fall. Loud noises can sometimes be heard coming from the ground.

Scientists estimate that more than one million earthquakes occur every year. This is approximately one earthquake every thirty seconds. The vast majority of earthquakes are so small that the surface of the Earth barely moves. Several thousand earthquakes a year move the surface of the Earth, however, in ways significant enough to notice. Several hundred earthquakes make major changes in the Earth's surface features. And about twenty earthquakes a year cause severe changes in the Earth's surface. It is this last group of earthquakes that has the potential to cause serious damage to buildings and dramatic loss of life in populated areas.

The most common cause of earthquakes is faulting. As you learned in Chapter 1, a fault is a break in the Earth's crust. During faulting, parts of the Earth's crust are pushed together or pulled apart. Rocks break and slide past one another. Energy is released during this process. As the rocks move, they cause nearby rocks to move also. The rocks continue to move in this way until the energy is used up.

Figure 2–1 *The damage brought about by the 1985 earthquake in Mexico City shows the awesome power of earthquake waves.*

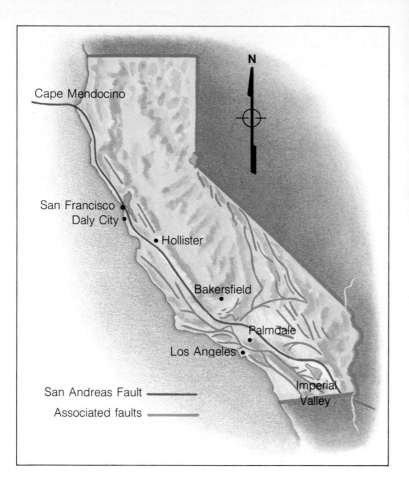

Figure 2–2 *The San Andreas Fault extends 960 kilometers along the western edge of California (left). Only a small portion of the fault is visible in the aerial photograph. However, you can see that movement along the fault has caused streams that run across the fault to become offset (top). Movement also causes rock formations to become buckled and twisted (bottom).*

The San Andreas Fault in California extends near the border with Mexico to the south through the city of San Francisco and continues on and off shore to the coast of northern California. The San Andreas Fault is about 960 kilometers long and 32 kilometers deep. The land to the west of the San Andreas Fault is slowly moving north. The land to the east of the fault is moving south. But the rocks along the fault do not all move at the same time. Eathquakes occur in one area and then in another. One of the worst of the disasters occurred in 1906, when movement along a small section of the San Andreas Fault caused the famous San Francisco earthquake.

Earthquakes also occur on the floor of the ocean. These earthquakes often produce giant sea waves called **tsunamis** (tsoo-NAH-meez). Tsunamis can travel at speeds of 700 to 800 kilometers per hour. As they approach the coast, tsunamis can reach heights of greater than 20 meters. To get a better idea of this

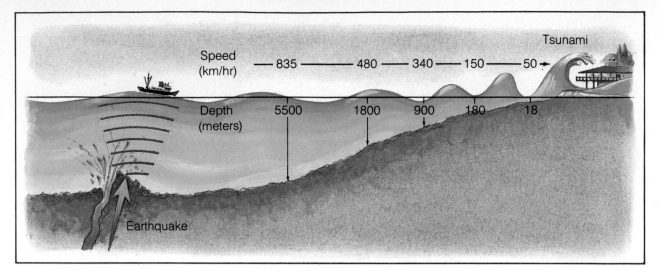

Figure 2–3 *Giant sea waves called tsunamis are caused by earthquakes on the ocean floor. When tsunamis are out at sea, they are far apart, fast moving, and low. What happens to these waves near shore?*

height, consider the following: A 6-story building is about 20 meters tall! When a tsunami strikes the coast, it can cause great damage.

Seismic Waves

Some faults are located deep inside the Earth. Others are close to or at the Earth's surface. Most faults occur between the surface and a depth of about 70 kilometers.

The point beneath the Earth's surface where the rocks break and move is called the **focus** (FOH-cuhs) of the earthquake. The focus is the underground point of origin of an earthquake. Directly above the focus, on the Earth's surface, is the **epicenter** (EHP-uh-sehn-tuhr). Earthquake waves reach the epicenter first. During an earthquake, the most violent shaking is found at the epicenter. See Figure 2–4.

Earthquake waves are known as **seismic** (SIGHZ-mihk) **waves.** Scientists have learned much about earthquakes and the interior of the Earth by studying seismic waves. There are three main types of seismic waves. Each type of wave has a characteristic speed and manner of travel.

PRIMARY WAVES Seismic waves that travel the fastest are called **primary waves,** or **P waves.** P waves arrive at a given point before any other type of seismic wave. P waves travel through solids, liquids, and

New Madrid, Missouri

If you think that earthquakes in the United States occur only along the San Andreas Fault in California, you are incorrect. During the years 1811 and 1812, a strong series of earthquakes occurred along the New Madrid Fault in southeastern Missouri and Arkansas.

You might enjoy reading about the New Madrid Fault. Begin with an article written by Robert Hamilton called "Quakes Along the Mississippi," published in the August 1980 edition of *Natural History* magazine.

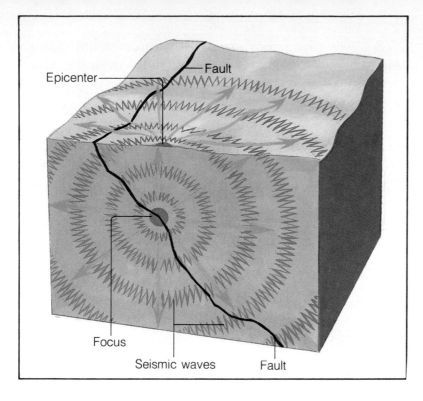

Epicenter — Fault

Focus

Seismic waves — Fault

Figure 2–4 *This diagram shows the relationship between the epicenter and the focus of an earthquake. Where do the strongest seismic waves occur?*

gases. They move through the Earth at different speeds, depending on the density of the material through which they are moving. As they move deeper into the Earth, where material is more dense, they speed up.

P waves are push-pull waves. As P waves travel, they push rock particles into the particles ahead of them, thus compressing the particles. The rock particles then bounce back. They hit the particles behind them that are being pushed forward. The particles move back and forth in the direction the waves are moving. See Figure 2–5.

SECONDARY WAVES Seismic waves that do not travel through the Earth as fast as P waves do are called **secondary waves,** or **S waves.** S waves arrive at a given point after P waves do. S waves travel through solids but not through liquids and gases. Like P waves, S waves speed up when they pass through denser material.

Part of the Earth's interior is molten, or a hot liquid. Because S waves do not travel through liquids, they are not always recorded at all locations during an earthquake. What happens to S waves when they reach the liquid part of the Earth's interior?

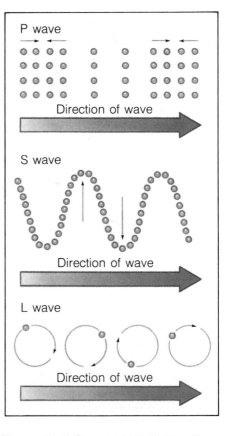

P wave

Direction of wave

S wave

Direction of wave

L wave

Direction of wave

Figure 2–5 *P waves push together and pull apart rock particles in the direction the waves are moving. S waves, which are slower than P waves, move rock particles from side to side at right angles to the direction the waves are moving. How do L waves move?*

FIND OUT BY CALCULATING

Graphing the Speed of a Tsunami

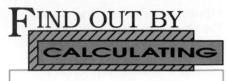

A tsunami far out to sea travels very quickly and carries a great deal of energy. Out at sea, however, tsunami waves are quite low. As a tsunami approaches shore, its speed decreases drastically, but it still carries the same amount of energy. What effect does the slowing down in speed have on the height of tsunami waves close to shore? Why are such waves so powerful?

Use the data from Figure 2–3 to make a graph plotting ocean depth against the speed of a tsunami. What general conclusions can you draw from your graph?

S waves cause rock particles to move from side to side. The rock particles move at right angles to the direction of the waves. See Figure 2–5.

SURFACE WAVES The slowest-moving seismic waves are called **surface waves,** or **L waves.** L waves arrive at a given point after primary and secondary waves do. L waves originate on the Earth's surface at the epicenter. Then they move along the Earth's surface the way waves travel in the ocean. Just as the water's surface rises and falls with each passing wave, the Earth's surface moves up and down with each L wave that passes. L waves cause most of the damage during an earthquake because they bend and twist the Earth's surface.

The Seismograph

A **seismograph** (SIGHZ-muh-grahf) is an instrument that detects and measures seismic waves. Although crude seismographs were in use hundreds of years ago, the first practical seismograph was developed by John Milne in 1893. Milne's invention has remained relatively unchanged to this day.

A seismograph consists of a weight attached to a spring or wire. See Figure 2–7. Because the weight is not attached directly to the Earth, it remains nearly still even when the Earth moves. A pen attached to the weight records any movement of the Earth on a sheet of paper wound around a constantly rotating drum.

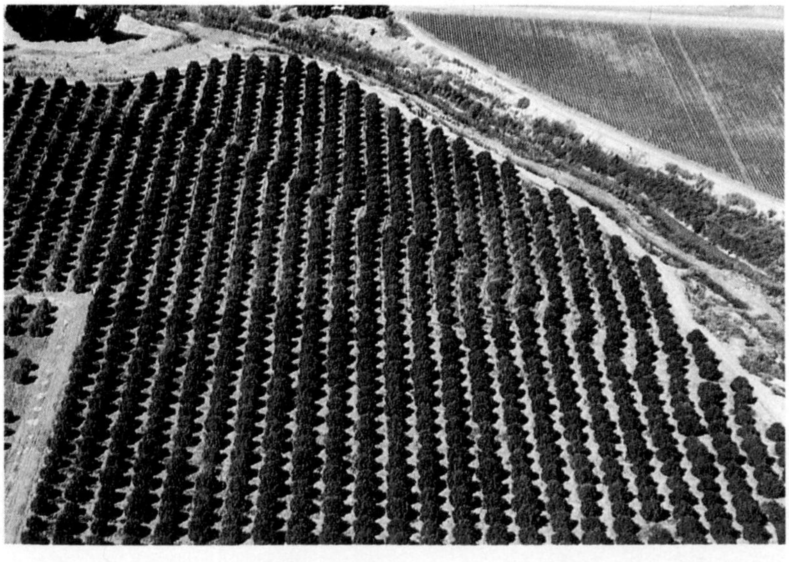

Figure 2–6 *Earthquakes can cause blocks of land to slip along a fault. How might such slippage affect railroad tracks, roads, and streams? How has slippage affected the straight rows of orange trees in the photograph?*

Because the pen is attached to the weight, it also remains nearly still when the Earth moves. But the drum moves with the Earth. When the Earth is still, the pen records a nearly straight line. When the Earth moves, the pen records a wavy line. What kind of line would be recorded during a violent earthquake?

Seismologists (sighz-MUHL-oh-jihstz), scientists who study earthquakes, can determine the strength of an earthquake by studying the height of the wavy lines recorded on the paper. The seismograph's record of waves is called a **seismogram** (SIGHZ-muh-gram). The higher the wavy lines on the seismogram are, the stronger the earthquake is.

In the past, the strength of an earthquake was estimated by observations of the visible destruction the earthquake caused. Scientists would inspect an area and "grade" the damage. They would then assign a number to the earthquake based on their observations. Today, the strength of earthquakes is measured on the **Richter scale**—a scale named after its creator, Charles Richter. The Richter scale measures the energy an earthquake releases by assigning the earthquake a number, traditionally from 1 to 10. The more energy an earthquake releases, the stronger it is. (Fortunately, up until now no earthquake has ever been graded a "perfect" 10!)

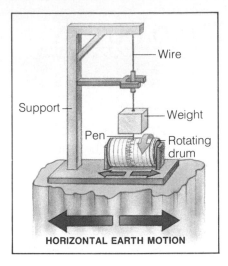

Figure 2–7 *In a seismograph, a heavy weight attached to a wire holds a pen motionless while a rotating drum moves with the Earth. What is a seismograph's record of seismic waves called?*

Figure 2–8 *In 1906, a devastating earthquake struck San Francisco. Fires that broke out after the earthquake destroyed part of the city (left). Buildings that normally stood straight and true were realigned by movements of the Earth (right).*

The Seismograph

Contact the geology department of a college or university near your home. Find out whether they have a working seismograph. If not, locate the nearest seismograph station that has one.

Arrange to visit the school or station with the seismograph. Observe it while it is working. Ask someone there how to read the seismogram—the recording sheet on the rotating drum.

Write a report about your trip and present it to your class.

Figure 2–9 *By finding out how much time it takes for a laser beam from a laser field station to strike a reflector and bounce back, scientists can accurately measure the movements along a fault.*

Each number on the Richter scale represents an earthquake stronger than an earthquake represented by the preceding number. Any number above 6 indicates a very destructive earthquake. As you might imagine, an earthquake assigned the number 10 would be truly devastating!

The amount of damage caused by an earthquake depends on several different factors. The earthquake's strength, the kind of rock and soil that underlies an area, the population of the area affected, the kinds of buildings in the area, and the time at which the earthquake occurs all influence how damaging a particular earthquake is.

Predicting Earthquakes

In their study of earthquakes, scientists hope to improve the ability to accurately predict them. To be useful, earthquake prediction must be reliable and complete. The prediction must include where, when, and how strong the earthquake will be. If a strong earthquake is predicted, people can be moved from areas in danger. In 1975, Chinese scientists predicted with great accuracy that an earthquake would occur in their country. Most of the people in three areas of the country were evacuated before the earthquake struck. Many thousands of lives were saved.

If strong earthquakes could be predicted years in advance, people could better plan the growth of cities. Buildings could be reinforced to better withstand the shock waves produced by an earthquake. In some cities, attempts have already been made to construct earthquake-proof buildings. In what other ways might more accurate earthquake prediction save lives?

Seismologists have identified some warning signals that help to predict earthquakes with greater accuracy. Often changes occur in the speeds of P waves and S waves before a major earthquake strikes. Sometimes slight changes in the tilt of the Earth's surface can be detected. Land near a fault may rise or sink slightly. The water level in wells often goes up or down. And although it sounds a bit unscientific, some scientists in China believe that changes in the behavior of certain animals might help to predict earthquakes.

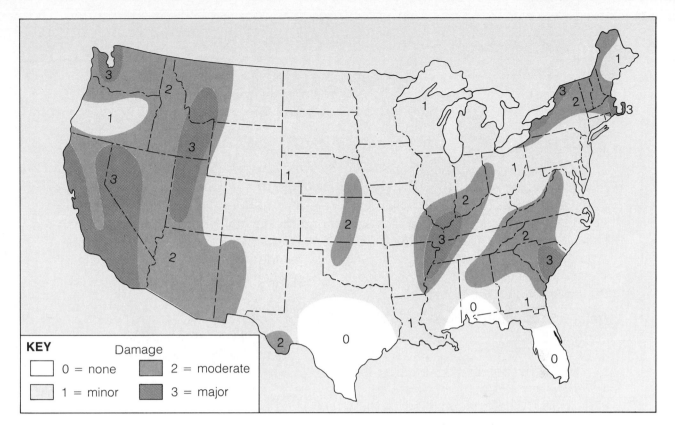

KEY

Damage

☐ 0 = none   ▨ 2 = moderate

▨ 1 = minor   ▧ 3 = major

Figure 2–10 *This Seismic Risk Map shows areas of the United States (excluding Alaska and Hawaii) where earthquakes are likely to occur and the relative damage they are likely to cause. Where are damaging earthquakes least likely to occur? Most likely to occur?*

2–1 Section Review

1. What is an earthquake? What is the most common cause of an earthquake?
2. What is the focus of an earthquake? The epicenter?
3. Describe the three major types of seismic waves.
4. How does a seismograph work?
5. How is the strength of an earthquake measured?

Critical Thinking—*Applying Concepts*

6. Two different cities experience earthquakes of similar strength. In one city, relatively few people are injured. In the other city, there is a great loss of life. What are some possible reasons for the different effects? What kinds of plans could be developed to limit earthquake damage in the future?

PROBLEM Solving

Shake, Quake, and Maybe Not Break

Cities built near fault zones in the crust face a serious problem. Their existence is threatened by the land upon which they are built. Architects and engineers constantly search for ways to construct buildings that will be better able to resist the movements of the Earth's crust that occur during an earthquake.

Relating Concepts

Pretend you are an architect or engineer planning an "earthquake-proof" building. What should your building look like? How should it be built? Where should it be built? What materials should you use? These are but a few of the questions to consider. Begin your project in the library, where you can find out about ideas of others who have tried to build earthquake-proof buildings. One student faced with this problem developed a plan for a building built on giant springs. What ideas can you and your classmates come up with?

2–2 Formation of a Volcano

Deep within the Earth, under tremendous pressure and at extreme temperatures, rock exists as a hot liquid called **magma**. This molten rock is found in pockets called magma chambers. Magma is constantly moving. In some places magma works its way toward the Earth's surface through cracks in solid rock. In other places, magma works its way toward the surface by melting the solid rock.

When magma reaches the Earth's surface, it is called **lava**. The place in the Earth's surface through which magma and other materials reach the surface (and the magma becomes lava) is called a **volcano.** You may have seen photographs of lava flowing down the sides of a volcano. A lava flow is so hot that it incinerates every burnable thing in its path. In some places, lava can build up to form a

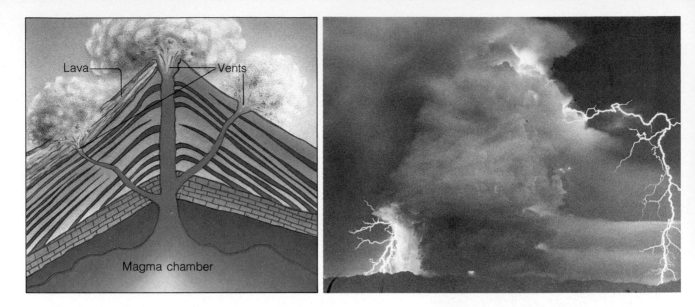

Lava — Vents

Magma chamber

cone-shaped mountain. Such a landform, which is the result of an accumulation of volcanic material, is often referred to as a volcano as well.

The opening from which lava erupts is called a **vent.** Volcanoes often have more than one vent. If there is more than one vent, lava will sometimes pour from the sides of a volcano as well as from the top.

Volcanic Eruptions

All volcanic eruptions are not alike. Some eruptions are quiet, with lava slowly oozing from a vent. Other eruptions are very violent, with lava and other materials being hurled hundreds of meters into the air. Gases from within the Earth's interior mix with huge quantities of volcanic dust and ash and rise into the air as great dark clouds that can be seen from many kilometers away. A violent volcanic eruption is truly an awesome sight.

Although it seems to be a dangerous endeavor, many scientists spend their working lives studying volcanoes. For volcanoes are "windows" into the interior of the Earth. By analyzing the mineral makeup of lava, geologists can determine the chemical composition of the magma from which the lava formed. Such data provide information about the composition of the part of the Earth that remains unseen. There are four main types of lava.

One type of lava is dark-colored and contains a lot of water. This lava is rich in the elements iron

Figure 2–11 *If you had been able to look inside Mount Pinatubo as it erupted in July 1991, you would have seen magma moving through the vents toward the Earth's surface.*

Figure 2–12 *Although you might not wish to touch lava with a "ten-foot pole," this potentially hazardous activity is all in a day's work for a volcanologist (scientist who studies volcanoes). The long pole contains a special probe that can measure the temperature of the lava.*

and magnesium. When this type of lava cools, igneous rocks such as basalt are formed. (You will learn more about rocks in Chapter 4.)

Another type of lava is light in color. This lava, which contains little water, is rich in the elements silicon and aluminum. Compounds of these elements account for its lighter color. When this type of lava cools, it forms the igneous rock rhyolite, which resembles granite.

The third type of lava has a chemical composition similar to that of both the dark-colored type and the light-colored type. Different varieties of igneous rocks in the Earth's crust, such as andesite, are formed from this type of lava.

The fourth type of lava contains large amounts of gases such as steam and carbon dioxide. When this lava hardens, it forms rocks with many holes in them. Like the holes trapped in the dough of a loaf of bread, the holes in this type of lava form as gas bubbles are trapped in the molten rock as it hardens. Pumice and scoria are igneous rocks formed from this type of lava. Do you know an unusual property of pumice?

Some dark-colored lava is thin and runny, and most tends to flow. The islands of Hawaii and Iceland were formed by many lava flows. But light-colored lava causes explosive eruptions. Because light-colored lava is rich in the element silicon, it tends to harden in the vents of a volcano. Explosive eruptions are caused when lava in the vents hardens into rocks. Steam and new lava build up under the rocks. When the pressure of the steam and new lava becomes great, a violent explosion occurs. As an example, if you place a cork in a bottle of seltzer water and shake the bottle, what do you think will happen? The cork will be pushed out of the bottle. The increased pressure exerted by the gas in the seltzer as a result of shaking the bottle causes the cork's ejection. This model illustrates what happens to a hardened lava plug in a vent as pressure builds up beneath it.

During volcanic eruptions, many rock fragments are blown into the air. The smallest particles are called **volcanic dust**. Particles of volcanic dust are very fine, less than 0.25 millimeter in diameter, or as tiny as grains of flour.

Figure 2–13 *There are two basic forms of dark-colored lava, both of which get their names from Hawaiian words. Hot, fast-flowing pahoehoe (pah-HOH-ay-hoh-ay) hardens into rounded swirls and ropy wrinkles (top). Cooler, slow-flowing aa (AH-ah) crumbles into large, jagged chunks as it oozes downhill. As a result, aa is rough and blocky (bottom). Can you explain why pahoehoe may change to aa as the lava moves away from the vent?*

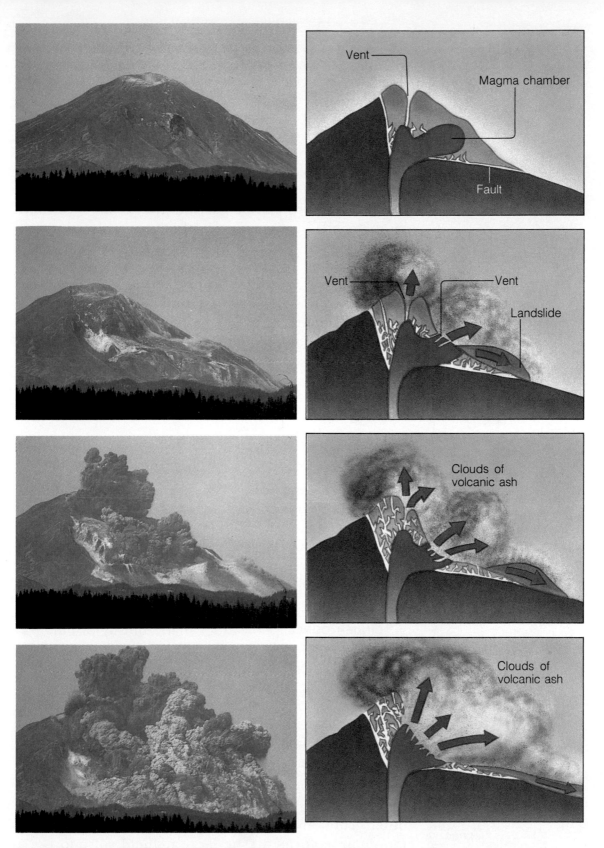

Figure 2–14 *In May 1980, Mount St. Helens in the state of Washington erupted explosively. These photographs and diagrams show the first few minutes of the eruption. What is the term for the openings from which lava erupts?*

Figure 2–15 *This car is covered with volcanic dust spewed from Mount Pinatubo in the Philippines. The effects of this natural disaster prove an irresistible attraction!*

CAREERS

Volcanologist

Volcanologists are interested in the origin of volcanoes, the kinds of materials volcanoes release, the different shapes volcanoes develop, and the causes of eruptions.

After graduating from college, many volcanologists teach, do research, or work for government organizations. To learn more about this career, write to the American Geophysical Union, 2000 Florida Avenue, NW, Washington, DC 20009.

Rock particles more than 0.25 millimeter but less than 5 millimeters in diameter are called **volcanic ash**. Particles of volcanic ash are about the size of rice grains. Volcanic ash falls to the Earth's surface and eventually forms small rocks. Both volcanic dust and volcanic ash can be carried away from a volcano by the wind. In this manner, they can fall to the Earth near the volcano, or they can be carried completely around the world.

Larger rock particles are called **volcanic bombs**. Volcanic bombs are a few centimeters to several meters in diameter. Some bombs are the size of boulders and have masses of several metric tons. Small volcanic bombs about the size of golf balls are called **cinders**. When volcanic bombs are hurled out of a volcano, they are molten. They harden as they travel through the air.

Types of Volcanoes

Different types of volcanic eruptions form different types of volcanoes. Some volcanoes are built from quiet flows of thin, runny lava that spread over a broad area. Other volcanoes are formed from violent eruptions. Some volcanoes are formed from a combination of quiet flows of lava and violent eruptions.

CINDER CONES Volcanoes made mostly of cinders and other rock particles that have been blown into the air are called **cinder cones**. Cinder cones form from explosive eruptions. Because the material in cinder cones is loosely arranged, the cones are not high. But they have a narrow base and steep sides. Paricutin in Mexico is a cinder cone.

SHIELD VOLCANOES Volcanoes composed of quiet lava flows are called **shield volcanoes**. Because it is runny, the lava flows over a large area. After several quiet eruptions, a gently sloping, dome-shaped mountain is formed. The largest shield volcano is Mauna Loa in the Hawaiian Islands. Mauna Loa rises from the bottom of the Pacific Ocean to a height of 4 kilometers above sea level.

CINDER CONE   SHIELD VOLCANO   COMPOSITE VOLCANO

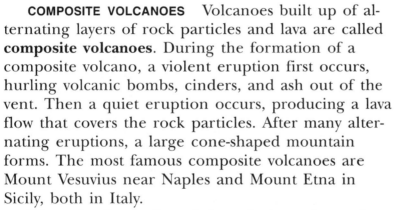

COMPOSITE VOLCANOES   Volcanoes built up of alternating layers of rock particles and lava are called **composite volcanoes**. During the formation of a composite volcano, a violent eruption first occurs, hurling volcanic bombs, cinders, and ash out of the vent. Then a quiet eruption occurs, producing a lava flow that covers the rock particles. After many alternating eruptions, a large cone-shaped mountain forms. The most famous composite volcanoes are Mount Vesuvius near Naples and Mount Etna in Sicily, both in Italy.

There is often a funnel-shaped pit or depression at the top of a volcanic cone. This pit is called a **crater.** If a crater becomes very large as a result of the collapse of its walls, it is called a **caldera**. A caldera may also form when the top of a volcano collapses or explodes. You may be familiar with the word caldron, a type of large cooking pot or kettle. The witches in *Macbeth*, a play written by William Shakespeare, stir their potions in a bubbling caldron. Both these words are derived from the Latin word *caldarius*, which pertains to warming. As you might guess, a volcano's caldera was at one time quite hot and contained bubbling lava.

Figure 2–16 *Izalco in El Salvador is a cinder cone (left). Kilauea in Hawaii is a shield volcano. The crater within the caldera is clearly visible (center). Mount Egmont in New Zealand is a composite volcano (right). How does a composite volcano form?*

FIND OUT BY
DOING

Making a Model Volcano

1. Use the diagrams in Figure 2–16 to make a papier-mâché model of a cross section of one of the three types of volcanoes.

2. Label the structures of your volcano. You might like to team up with other students to make sure that a model of each type is constructed.

Figure 2–17 *Volcanic cones often have a depression known as a crater at their summit. Locate the craters of these two Indonesian volcanoes. Why is the crater of the volcano in the back considered to be quite unusual? In general, if a crater is more than three times wider than it is deep, it is called a caldera. Craters and calderas may fill with water to form lakes.*

Volcanic Activity

Volcanoes are rather unpredictable phenomena. Some volcanoes erupt fairly regularly; others have not erupted within modern history. In order to indicate the relative activity of volcanoes, scientists classify them as active, dormant, or extinct.

An active volcano is one that erupts either continually or periodically. There are several active volcanoes in the continental United States: Lassen Peak in Lassen Volcanic National Park (California), Mount St. Helens in the Cascade Range (Washington State), and Mount Katmai (Alaska).

A volcano that has been known to erupt within modern times but is now inactive is classified as a dormant, or "sleeping," volcano. Mount Ranier (Washington State), Mount Hood (Oregon), and Mount Shasta (California) are examples of dormant volcanoes in the continental United States.

A volcano not known to have erupted within modern history is classified as an extinct volcano. Volcanologists (scientists who study volcanoes) consider truly extinct volcanoes to be only those that have been worn away almost to the level of their magma chamber. But even so-called extinct volcanoes can prove unpredictable. Both Lassen Peak and Mount St. Helens suddenly erupted after long periods of inactivity.

FIND OUT BY

Volcano in Motion

1. Using eight to ten unlined note cards, draw each successive step in the movement of magma up and out of a volcano. Use Figures 2–11 and 2–14 as guides and use your imagination.

2. Number each note card in sequence as you draw it.

3. Tape the cards together along the top.

Hold the cards at the taped end and flip from the first card to the last card.

2–2 Section Review

1. What is a volcano? What determines the type of volcano formed? Describe the three types of volcanoes.
2. What is the difference between magma and lava?
3. List in order of increasing size the different kinds of particles blown from a volcano.
4. How are volcanoes classified according to activity?

Connection—*Ecology*

5. How does a volcanic eruption alter the area around a volcano? What changes in plant and animal life do you think you would notice in the area around a volcano that has just erupted?

2–3 Volcano and Earthquake Zones

Guide for Reading

Focus on this question as you read.

▶ *Where are volcano and earthquake zones located?*

Have you ever wondered why California seems to have more than its share of earthquakes? Or why there are so many active volcanoes on islands in the Pacific Ocean? Volcanic eruptions and earthquakes often occur in the same areas of the world. Sometimes volcanic eruptions are accompanied by earthquakes. Although the two events need not occur together, there is a relationship between their occurrences. **Most major earthquakes and volcanic eruptions occur in three zones of the world. Scientists believe that there is a great deal of movement and activity in the Earth's crust in these zones**. You may want to look at a map of the world as you read about these zones. It is helpful to locate the places you read about on a map so that they become more "real" to you.

One major earthquake and volcano zone extends nearly all the way around the edge of the Pacific Ocean. This zone goes through New Zealand, the Philippines, Japan, Alaska, and along the western coasts of North and South America. The San Andreas Fault is part of this zone. This zone that circles the Pacific Ocean is called the **Ring of Fire**. Can you explain how it got its name?

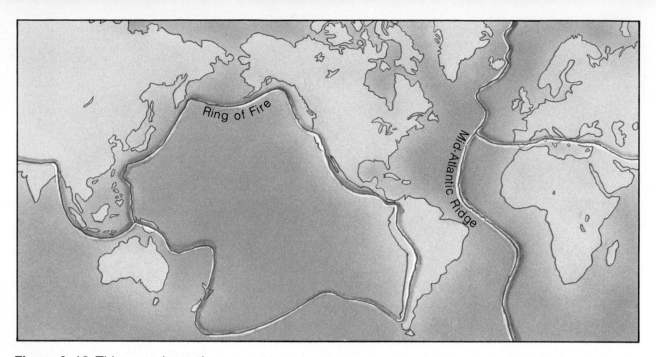

Figure 2–18 *This map shows the Ring of Fire, a zone of earthquake and volcanic activity that surrounds the Pacific Ocean. What is the name of the earthquake and volcano zone at the bottom of the Atlantic Ocean?*

A second major earthquake and volcano zone is located near the Mediterranean Sea. This zone, called the Mediterranean Zone, extends across Asia into India. Many countries in the zone, including Italy, Greece, and Turkey, have violent earthquakes. Many volcanic eruptions have also occurred in this zone.

The third major earthquake and volcano zone extends through Iceland to the middle of the Atlantic Ocean. There is under the ocean a long range of volcanic mountains called the Mid-Atlantic Ridge. Scientists believe that the volcano and earthquake activity in this area are due to the formation of new parts of the Earth's crust along the ridge. Volcanic islands in the Atlantic Ocean, such as Iceland, are part of the Mid-Atlantic Ridge.

2–3 Section Review

1. Why are earthquake and volcano activity zones located in certain areas?
2. What is the Ring of Fire?
3. What do scientists believe causes so many earthquakes in the middle of the Atlantic Ocean?

Critical Thinking—*Relating Concepts*
4. Would a volcanic eruption be likely to occur on the east coast of the United States? Explain.

The Vault of the Earth

Naples is a large sun-filled city in southern Italy. But stand in many places in the city and you are immediately aware that a dark shadow looms overhead. Across the Bay of Naples, Mount Vesuvius, an active volcano, rises to a height of 1220 meters. By world standards, Mount Vesuvius is neither very large nor very old. But it played an important role in the history of the Mediterranean region.

On August 24, AD 79, life in two ancient cities, Pompeii and Herculaneum, abruptly came to an end with the eruption of Mount Vesuvius. Pompeii was covered with a layer of fine, hot ash—a layer that trapped people and animals and preserved ancient buildings and household furnishings. Herculaneum was covered by a river of mud that contained pumice spewed forth from the volcano. Not until the eighteenth and nineteenth centuries did *archaeologists,* scientists who study the remains of past civilizations, become aware of the treasures preserved by Vesuvius's anger.

The layer of ash that covered Pompeii made casts of people frantically trying to escape the eruption. Most people died when the hot ash in the air entered their lungs, choking off a fresh supply of oxygen. The people of Herculaneum were luckier. Although their city was destroyed, they were able to flee the slow-moving mud slides.

Thus the eruption of Vesuvius, while it destroyed two lively cities of the ancient world, preserved evidence of these civilizations for almost two thousand years. Scientists are now able to study a great historical treasure preserved in a vault made from materials spewed forth during a devastating volcanic eruption.

Laboratory Investigation

Locating Patterns of Earthquake and Volcano Distribution

Problem

What is the worldwide pattern of earthquake and volcano distribution?

Materials (per student)

world map showing longitude and latitude
4 pencils of different colors

Procedure

1. Use the information in the table to plot the location of each earthquake. Use one of the colored pencils to label on the world map each earthquake location with the letter E inside a circle.

2. Do the same thing for volcanoes. Use another colored pencil and the letter V inside a circle.

3. Use another pencil to lightly shade the areas in which earthquakes are found.

4. Use another pencil to lightly shade the areas in which volcanoes are found.

Observations

1. Are earthquakes scattered randomly over the surface of the Earth or are they concentrated in definite zones?

2. Are volcanoes scattered randomly or concentrated in definite zones?

3. Are most earthquakes and volcanoes located near the edges or near the center of continents?

4. Are there any active volcanoes near your home? Has an earthquake occurred near your home?

Analysis and Conclusions

1. Describe any patterns you observed in the distribution of earthquakes and volcanoes.

2. What relationship exists between the locations of earthquakes and of volcanoes?

3. **On Your Own** On a map of the United States, locate active volcanoes and areas of earthquake activity in the fifty states.

EARTHQUAKES		VOLCANOES	
Longitude	Latitude	Longitude	Latitude
120°W	40°N	150°W	60°N
110°E	5°S	70°W	35°S
77°W	4°S	120°W	45°N
88°E	23°N	61°W	15°N
121°E	14°S	105°W	20°N
34°E	7°N	75°W	0°
74°W	44°N	122°W	40°N
70°W	30°S	30°E	40°N
10°E	45°N	60°E	30°N
85°W	13°N	160°E	55°N
125°E	23°N	37°E	3°S
30°E	35°N	145°E	40°N
140°E	35°N	120°E	10°S
12°E	46°N	14°E	41°N
75°E	28°N	105°E	5°S
150°W	61°N	35°E	15°N
68°W	47°S	70°W	30°S

Summarizing Key Concepts

2–1 Earthquakes

▲ An earthquake is the shaking and trembling that results from the sudden movement of part of the Earth's crust.

▲ The most common cause of earthquakes is faulting.

▲ Giant sea waves called tsunamis are caused by earthquakes on the ocean floor.

▲ The underground point of origin of an earthquake is called the focus.

▲ The epicenter is located on the Earth's surface directly above the focus.

▲ Earthquake waves are called seismic waves. There are three types of seismic waves: primary (P), secondary (S), and surface (L) waves.

▲ Seismic waves are detected and measured by a seismograph.

▲ The strength of an earthquake is measured on the Richter scale.

2–2 Formation of a Volcano

▲ Magma that reaches the Earth's surface is called lava.

▲ The place where magma reaches the Earth's surface is called a volcano.

▲ The opening from which lava erupts is called a vent.

▲ The mineral makeup of lava provides a clue to the chemical composition of magma inside the Earth.

▲ Many rock fragments of varying sizes are blown into the air during volcanic eruptions. They include volcanic dust, volcanic ash, volcanic bombs, and cinders.

▲ Different types of volcanic eruptions form different types of volcanoes. These include cinder cones, shield volcanoes, and composite volcanoes.

2–3 Volcano and Earthquake Zones

▲ There are three major earthquake and volcano zones in the world where a great deal of movement in the Earth's crust occurs.

▲ The funnel-shaped pit, or depression, at the top of a volcano cone is called a crater. A caldera forms when the walls of a crater collapse.

Reviewing Key Terms

Define each term in a complete sentence.

2–1 Earthquakes

earthquake
tsunami
focus
epicenter
seismic wave
primary wave, P wave
secondary wave, S wave
surface wave, L wave
seismograph
seismologist
seismogram
Richter scale

2–2 Formation of a Volcano

magma
lava
volcano
vent
volcanic dust
volcanic ash
volcanic bomb
cinder
cinder cone
shield volcano
composite volcano
crater
caldera

2–3 Volcano and Earthquake Zones

Ring of Fire

Chapter Review

Content Review

Multiple Choice

Choose the letter of the answer that best completes each statement.

1. The most common cause of earthquakes is
   a. tsunamis.   c. seismic waves.
   b. faulting.   d. magma.
2. Giant sea waves caused by earthquakes on the ocean floor are called
   a. volcanoes.   c. seismograms.
   b. faults.   d. tsunamis.
3. The underground point of origin of an earthquake is the
   a. focus.   c. magma.
   b. epicenter.   d. lava.
4. During an earthquake, the most violent shaking occurs at the
   a. Ring of Fire.   c. focus.
   b. epicenter.   d. vent.
5. The fastest seismic waves are
   a. S waves.   c. V waves.
   b. L waves.   d. P waves.
6. The seismic waves that cause most of the damage during an earthquake are
   a. S waves.   c. V waves.
   b. L waves.   d. P waves.
7. The instrument used to detect and measure earthquake waves is called the
   a. seismograph.   c. voltmeter.
   b. seismogram.   d. barometer.
8. The scale used to measure the strength of an earthquake is the
   a. focus scale.
   b. Milne scale.
   c. Richter scale.
   d. San Andreas scale.
9. Hot liquid rock that is found in the interior of the Earth is called
   a. lava.   c. ash.
   b. magma.   d. cinders.
10. The largest rock fragments blown into the air during a volcanic eruption are
    a. volcanic ash.
    b. volcanic dust.
    c. volcanic cinders.
    d. volcanic bombs.

True or False

If the statement is true, write "true." If it is false, change the underlined word or words to make the statement true.

1. A <u>caldera</u> forms when the walls of a volcano crater collapse.
2. The <u>Ring of Fire</u> is a zone of volcano activity that surrounds the Pacific Ocean.
3. <u>Secondary</u> waves travel through solids but not through liquids.
4. The opening from which lava erupts is called a <u>fault</u>.
5. Small volcanic bombs are called <u>craters</u>.
6. Volcanoes composed of quiet lava flows are called <u>shield volcanoes</u>.
7. A funnel-shaped pit at the top of a volcanic cone is called a <u>vent</u>.

Concept Mapping

Complete the following concept map for Section 2–1. Refer to pages J6–J7 to construct a concept map for the entire chapter.

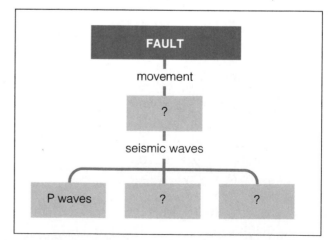

Concept Mastery

Discuss each of the following in a brief paragraph.

1. What is an earthquake? What is the most common cause of earthquakes?
2. Explain the difference between the focus of an earthquake and the epicenter of an earthquake.
3. What are seismic waves? Why are L waves more destructive than P or S waves?
4. What is the Richter scale? How is this scale used to compare earthquakes?

5. What is a volcano?
6. Describe the differences in the four kinds of lava.
7. Compare the shape and method of formation of cinder cones, shield volcanoes, and composite volcanoes.
8. Volcanoes are classified as active, dormant, or extinct. What do these classifications mean?

Critical Thinking and Problem Solving

Use the skills you have developed in this chapter to answer each of the following.

1. **Relating cause and effect** In 1883, the island of Krakatoa in the Pacific Ocean was destroyed by a tremendous volcanic explosion. Huge amounts of volcanic dust were hurled into the air. This dust remained in the air for several years before settling to the Earth. As far away as Europe scientists noted that temperatures dropped. Several years were referred to as "years without summers." Explain why this was so.

2. **Relating concepts** The Richter scale is used to rate the relative strength of earthquakes. How many times stronger than an earthquake rated 3 on the Richter scale is an earthquake rated 6? What are the advantages of using a single scale to rate the relative strengths of all earthquakes?
3. **Applying concepts** Earthquakes and volcanic eruptions occur naturally in certain zones. Does this mean that an earthquake or a volcanic eruption cannot occur outside one of these zones? What kinds of conditions would be necessary for an earthquake or volcanic eruption to occur outside these zones?
4. **Identifying relationships** In Section 2–2 you read about the formation of igneous rocks. The word igneous comes from a Latin word that means fire. What is the relationship between volcanoes and igneous rocks?
5. **Using the writing process** Pretend that you are a reporter for the *Daily Roman,* working in 79 AD. You are on assignment in Pompeii when Mount Vesuvius erupts. Write a dispatch for your newspaper describing your observations.

Plate Tectonics

Guide for Reading

After you read the following sections, you will be able to

3–1 Earth's Drifting Continents
- Describe the evidence for the theory of continental drift.

3–2 Earth's Spreading Ocean Floor
- Relate ocean-floor spreading to continental drift.

3–3 Earth's Moving Plates
- Discuss the theory of plate tectonics.

Have you ever looked at a globe or world map and noticed that the Earth's landmasses resemble pieces of a giant jigsaw puzzle? For example, the east coast of South America matches up with the west coast of Africa. The Arabian Peninsula and the northeast coast of Africa also seem to fit together.

Since the 1600s, people have wondered why the Earth's landmasses look like they would fit together. Were they connected at one time? If so, how were they moved apart?

In time, new discoveries caused other questions about the Earth to be asked. Why do places far from one another and with different climates have the remains of the same types of ancient organisms? Why do mountains and valleys form where they do? Why do earthquakes and volcanoes occur in the same areas over and over again?

For many years, no one came up with a theory that provided satisfactory answers. Then in 1915, a young German scientist published a radical, extremely controversial new theory. Read on, and discover more about the development of a theory that put the pieces of the puzzle together and revealed a better picture of the dynamic planet on which we live.

Journal *Activity*

You and Your World Have you ever been in a situation in which you knew you were right, but no one would listen to you? In your journal, describe the situation and how it made you feel.

◄ *This photograph taken from space shows that the Arabian Peninsula (top) and northeastern Africa (bottom) look as if they are two pieces of a giant puzzle.*

FIND OUT BY DOING

Putting the Pieces Together

1. Find one or two friends who also want to do this activity.

2. Obtain one sheet of newspaper per person. (Make sure you use a paper that everyone has finished reading!)

3. Tear a sheet of newspaper into a few large pieces.

4. Trade pieces with a friend.

5. Try to fit the pieces together. How do lines of print help to confirm that you have reassembled the pieces correctly?

■ How does this activity relate to the development of the theory of continental drift?

3–1 Earth's Drifting Continents

Imagine that you are browsing in the library, looking for something interesting to read. A paper on prehistoric plants and animals catches your eye, and you start to look through it. But partway through, you put the paper down and start to think. The theory presented in the paper does not sound right to you.

This is the theory: A land bridge once stretched across the Atlantic Ocean and connected South America and Africa. Evidence for this land bridge is seen in the **fossils** of plants and animals that could not possibly have crossed an ocean but are found in both South America and Africa. Fossils are the preserved remains of ancient organisms.

The author of the paper states that the land bridge no longer exists because it sank to the bottom of the ocean. Knowing what you do about isostasy, you realize that continental crust cannot sink into denser oceanic crust. Why, then, are the fossils the same on both sides of the Atlantic Ocean?

Suddenly, you realize that South America and Africa must have been connected at one time—but not in the way the author of the paper envisioned. You remember noticing how well the coasts of the two continents fit together and wondering if they had once been a single landmass. At the time, you thought that idea was silly. Now it seems to be an idea worth considering.

You begin to search through the reference materials in the library, looking for evidence that will support or disprove your hypothesis. The more research you do, the more evidence you find in favor of your hypothesis: **The Earth once had a single landmass that broke up into large pieces, which have since drifted apart.** You name this giant landmass of the distant past **Pangaea** (pan-JEE-ah), which means all Earth.

This story is based on real events that happened in the first half of this century to the German scientist Alfred Wegener. Wegener was not the first person to suggest that the continents had once been joined together and had since moved apart. However, he was the first to build a detailed scientific case in support of the idea.

Wegener's **theory of continental drift** contradicted many of the existing, widely-accepted ideas about the evolution of the Earth. At that time, scientists thought that the crust could not move horizontally—continents were permanently fixed in the positions in which they had formed billions of years before. As you can imagine, most established scientists reacted unfavorably to being told many basic principles of geology were incorrect—especially by a young man who was not even a geologist! Wegener, you see, was a meteorologist, or weather scientist. Wegener's theory was met with great hostility and rejected by most of the world's scientists.

Despite the extremely negative response of most of the world's scientists, Wegener and his supporters continued to believe in the theory of continental drift. They kept on collecting evidence to support the theory. About thirty years after Wegener's death, enough evidence had been gathered to convince almost all scientists that continental drift was an acceptable, useful theory.

Evidence From Fossils

Evidence from fossils supports Wegener's theory of continental drift. As you read earlier, Wegener began to work seriously on the theory when he read that identical types of fossils had been found in Africa and South America. But as you can see in Figure 3–1, fossils reveal connections among other continents as well.

One organism whose fossils provide evidence for continental drift is *Glossopteris* (glahs-SAHP-teh-rihs), an extinct, or no longer living, plant.

Glossopteris fossils, which are located in rocks about 250 million years old, are found in South Africa, Australia, India, and Antarctica. *Glossopteris* seeds were too large to have been carried by wind and too fragile to have survived a trip by ocean waves. The seeds could not possibly have traveled the great distances that separate the continents today. This suggests that the places in which the plant's fossils are found must once have been closer together.

Figure 3–1 *The fossilized leaves of the extinct plant* Glossopteris *have been found in southern Africa, Australia, India, and Antarctica. Today, these places are widely separated and have different climates. What do the* Glossopteris *fossils indicate about the positions of the continents in the past?*

Figure 3–2 *Continental drift helped to explain a biological mystery: why green sea turtles living near the coast of Brazil lay their eggs on a distant island in the middle of the Atlantic Ocean. Long ago, before Africa and South America moved further apart, this island was quite close to Brazil.*

The presence of *Glossopteris* fossils in the frozen wastelands of Antarctica indicates that Anarctica's climate millions of years ago was far different from the way it is today. Because the size and location of landmasses have a powerful effect on climate, this suggests that Antarctica and the other continents have changed position.

How did *Glossopteris* develop on such widely separated continents? Like Wegener, scientists today think that *Glossopteris* and many other organisms of the distant past lived on a single landmass—Pangaea. This landmass later split apart. The pieces of the broken landmass—today's continents—slowly drifted away from one another, carrying their fossils with them.

Evidence From Rocks

You have just read how fossils, which are located within rocks, provide support for the theory of continental drift. But fossils are not the only evidence for continental drift. The rocks themselves indicate that the continents have drifted.

One of the clearest sets of evidence is found in the rocks of Africa and South America. When the continents are "pieced" together, rock formations in Africa line up with matching ones in South America. An ancient folded mountain chain that stretches across South Africa links up with an equally ancient folded mountain chain in Argentina. Coal fields with distinctive layers in Brazil line up with coal fields with identical layers in Africa. And there are many other matches. Can you explain how these matching rock formations ended up on opposite sides of an ocean?

Rock deposits left behind by moving sheets of ice known as glaciers have also been used as evidence to support the theory of continental drift. Many glacial deposits are found in South America, Africa, India, Australia, and Antarctica. The similarity of these deposits indicates that they were left by the same ice sheets.

Many of these ancient glacial deposits have been found in areas with very warm climates. Because glaciers usually form close to the poles, scientists have concluded that these areas were once part of a giant landmass located near the South Pole.

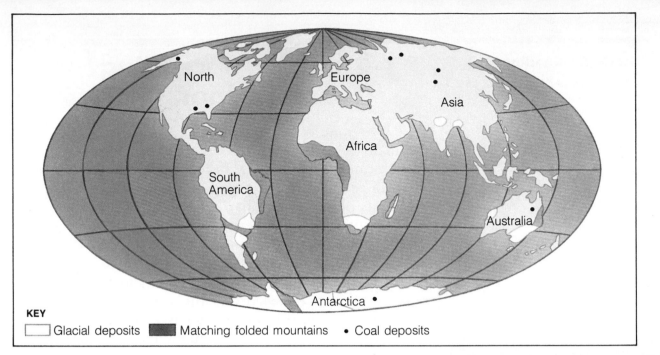

KEY

☐ Glacial deposits ■ Matching folded mountains • Coal deposits

Other kinds of rock deposits—including salts, coal, and limestone derived from coral reefs—also provide evidence of changes in climate caused by continental drift. Today most salt deposits form in areas between 10° and 35° north and south of the equator. But salt deposits hundreds of millions of years old have been found as far north as Michigan. Coal forms in warm, swampy climates. Yet large coal deposits have been discovered in Antarctica. And limestone deposits from coral reefs, which form in tropical climates, have been found in western Texas, the northern central United States, and other places far from the equator.

Figure 3–3 *The map shows some of the matching rock formations, which indicate the continents were once joined together and have since moved apart. Red sandstone, which makes up this arch in Utah, is formed only in deserts near the equator. What does this imply about the location of Utah in the past?*

3–1 Section Review

1. What is continental drift? Who first developed a scientific argument for continental drift?
2. How do scientists explain the existence of fossils of the same plants and animals on continents thousands of kilometers apart?

Critical Thinking—*Evaluating Theories*

3. "Wegener's lack of formal training in geology helped him to develop the theory of continental drift, but hurt him in getting his ideas accepted." What is the reasoning behind this statement? Do you agree? Why or why not?

3–2 Earth's Spreading Ocean Floor

In spite of all the evidence from fossils and rocks, many scientists still refused to accept the theory of continental drift. They were waiting for the answer to a very important question: How could the continents plow through hard, solid ocean floor?

Until recently, there was no acceptable answer to this question. Then, during the 1950s and 1960s, new techniques and instruments enabled scientists to make better observations of the ocean floor. These observations revealed that the continents do not plow through the ocean floor like ships in an icy sea. How the continents actually move is far stranger.

New mapping techniques gave scientists a much clearer picture of the ocean floor. They discovered a large system of underwater mountains that have a deep crack, called a rift valley, running through their center. These underwater mountains are known as **midocean ridges.** What do you think is the name of the ridge in the Atlantic Ocean?

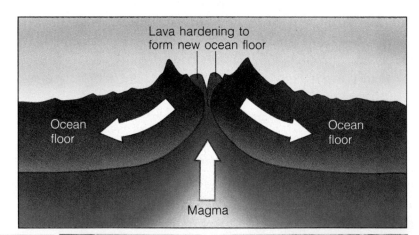

Figure 3–4 *As the ocean floor moves away from the midocean ridge, lava flows out of the rift and hardens to form new ocean floor. The island of Iceland was formed when part of the Mid-Atlantic Ridge rose above the surface of the ocean. Why does this big crack run through the center of Iceland? Why does Iceland have a lot of volcanic activity?*

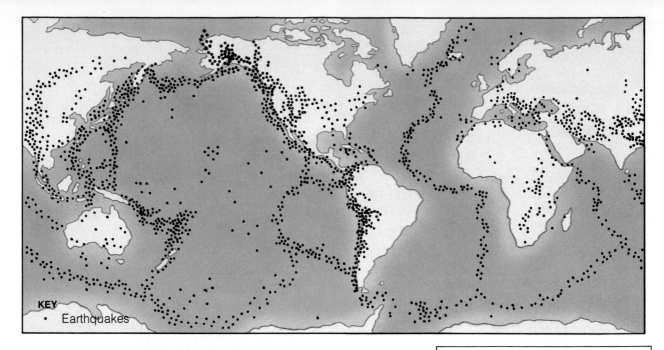

KEY
• Earthquakes

The midocean ridges form the single largest mountain chain in the world. The chain is approximately 80,000 kilometers long—roughly twenty times the distance from Los Angeles to New York City—and 3 kilometers high.

A great deal of volcanic activity occurs at the midocean ridges. Lava erupts from the rift valley that runs the length of a ridge. As the ocean floor moves away on either side of the ridge lava wells up and hardens. The hardened lava forms new ocean floor. This process is called **ocean-floor spreading.** So the ocean floor that scientists once thought was solid and immovable actually can move! **Ocean-floor spreading helps to explain how continents drift.** As a piece of the ocean floor moves, it takes its continent (if it has one) with it.

Although individual sections of midocean ridges are perfectly straight, the ridges as a whole curve. This is because the straight ridge sections are offset by thin cracks known as **transform faults.** Recall from Chapter 1 that a fault is a break or crack in the Earth's crust along which movement occurs. Look at Figure 3–5. Can you explain why a lot of earthquakes take place at the midocean ridges?

New deep-sea drilling machines also provided evidence to support the idea of ocean-floor spreading. Rock samples from the ocean floor indicate that rocks next to a midocean ridge are younger than rocks farther away. The youngest rocks are in the

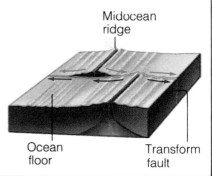

Midocean ridge

Ocean floor

Transform fault

Figure 3–5 *The diagram shows how sections of ocean floor move along a transform fault. The map shows where earthquakes took place over a seven-year period. Why were scientists able to locate midocean ridges by looking for areas with lots of earthquakes?*

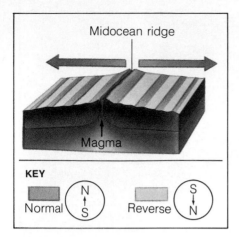

Midocean ridge

Magma

KEY

Normal | N/S
Reverse | S/N

Figure 3–6 *Reversals of the Earth's magnetic poles are recorded in the rocks of the ocean floor. Because the periods of normal and reverse poles are not equal in length, the magnetic stripes in the rocks vary in width. The pattern of stripes is identical on both sides of a midocean ridge. How are these matching stripes evidence of ocean-floor spreading?*

FIND OUT BY READING

Worlds Apart

What will the Earth look like in the future? How will the continuing evolution of Earth's surface affect the evolution of Earth's living things? For one person's vision of the Earth of the distant future, read *After Man* by Dougal Dixon.

center of the ridge. As the ocean floor spreads, the older rocks move farther away from the ridge.

Magnetic stripes in ocean-floor rocks further convinced scientists of ocean-floor spreading. Scientists know that some minerals have magnetic properties and are affected by the Earth's magnetism. In molten rock, the magnetic mineral particles line up in the direction of the Earth's magnetic poles. When the molten rock hardens, a permanent record of the Earth's magnetism remains in the rocks. Scientists discovered that the history of the Earth's magnetism is recorded in magnetic stripes in the rocks. Although these stripes cannot be seen, they can be detected by special instruments. What, scientists wondered, caused these stripes to form?

When scientists studied the magnetic stripes, they made a surprising discovery. The Earth's magnetic poles reverse themselves from time to time. In other words, the magnetic north and south poles change places. Studies show that during the past 3.5 million years, the magnetic poles have reversed themselves nine times.

But the scientists were in for an even bigger surprise. As you can see in Figure 3–6, the pattern of magnetic stripes is identical on both sides of a midocean ridge. In other words, the pattern of magnetic stripes on one side of a ridge matches the pattern on the other side. The obvious conclusion was that as magma hardens into rock at a midocean ridge, half the rock moves in one direction and the other half moves in the other direction. The pattern of magnetic stripes provides clear evidence of ocean-floor spreading.

You might think that as a result of ocean-floor spreading, the Earth's surface is getting larger. But this is definitely not the case. Just what is going on, then? Here's some information that might help you answer this question. The oldest rocks on land are almost 4 billion years old. But the oldest rocks on the ocean floor are only 200 million years old.

Because the Earth's surface remains the same size, the ocean floor is being destroyed as fast as it is being formed by ocean-floor spreading. This would explain why the rocks on the ocean floor are so young—all the old ocean floor has been destroyed. But how does this destruction occur?

The answer involves deep, V-shaped valleys called **trenches** that lie along the bottom of the oceans. The trenches are the deepest parts of the oceans. They are found close to the continents or near strings of islands such as Alaska's Aleutian Islands. The Pacific Ocean has many trenches around its edges. Can you explain why the location of these trenches is significant? (*Hint:* Look back at Section 2–3.)

As you learned earlier, older ocean floor moves away from the midocean ridges as new ocean floor is formed. Eventually, the older ocean floor moves down deep into the Earth along the trenches. The process in which crust plunges back into the Earth is called **subduction** (suhb-DUHK-shuhn).

When the rocks are pushed deep enough, they are melted by the heat of the Earth. Some of the molten rock will rise up through the crust and produce volcanoes. But most of the molten rock will become part of the mantle. (Recall from Chapter 1 that the mantle is the layer of the Earth that extends from the bottom of the crust downward to the core.) So as new rocks are formed along the midocean ridges, older rocks are subducted into the trenches. One process balances the other. The Earth's crust remains the same size.

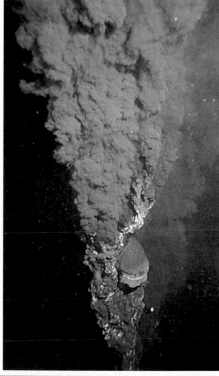

Figure 3–7 *The diagram shows how ocean floor is created and destroyed during ocean-floor spreading. What happens to the ocean floor at a midocean ridge? At a trench? The photograph shows water, cloudy with dissolved chemicals and heated by underlying magma, rising from a vent on a ridge in the eastern Pacific Ocean.*

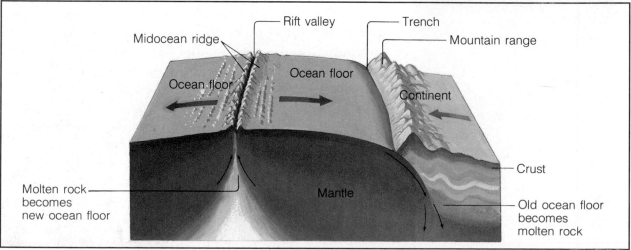

3–2 Section Review

1. What process helps explain how continents drift?
2. Where are the youngest rocks on the ocean floor found?

Critical Thinking—*Relating Concepts*

3. How can the magnetic orientation of rocks be used to trace the way a continent moved as it drifted? (*Hint:* Special techniques exist for determining the age of rocks.)

Guide for Reading

Focus on these questions as you read.

▶ *What is the theory of plate tectonics?*

▶ *How do plate movements relate to various features of the Earth?*

3–3 Earth's Moving Plates

By the 1960s, it had become clear that the Earth was far more dynamic than people had once believed. The overwhelming evidence for continental drift and ocean-floor spreading caused many of the old theories about the Earth to be discarded. A new theory about the evolution of the Earth began to develop. In time, this new theory was named the **theory of plate tectonics** (tehk-TAHN-ihks). The word **plate** refers to the moving, irregularly-shaped slabs that fit together like paving stones to form the surface layer of the Earth. The plates carry the continents and are edged by trenches and ridges. The word **tectonics** refers to the branch of geology that deals with the movements that shape the Earth's crust. **The theory of plate tectonics, which links together the ideas of continental drift and ocean-floor spreading, explains how the Earth has evolved over time. It helps to explain the formation, movements, collisions, and destruction of the Earth's crust.**

The theory of plate tectonics provides a framework for understanding mountains, volcanoes, earthquakes, and other landforms and processes of the physical Earth. It also gives scientists insight into how and why life on Earth has evolved. Like all good scientific theories, the theory of plate tectonics helps people to understand the past and to predict the future.

Lithospheric Plates

According to the theory of plate tectonics, the topmost solid part of the Earth, called the **lithosphere** (LIHTH-oh-sfeer), is made of a number of plates. The plates contain a thin layer of crust above a thick layer of relatively cool, rigid mantle rock. Plates usually contain both oceanic and continental crust.

There are seven major lithospheric plates, each of which is named after its surface features. The Pacific plate, which covers one-fifth of the Earth's surface, is the largest plate. The other major plates are the North American, South American, Eurasian, African, Indo-Australian, and Antarctic plates. Can you locate the seven major plates in Figure 3–8?

There are also many smaller plates. Some of these, such as the Caribbean and Arabian plates, are fairly large. Others are so small that they are not included in maps that show the entire Earth.

Plates move at different speeds and in different directions. Some small plates that lack landmasses move as much as several centimeters per year. Large plates that are weighted down with continents move only a few millimeters per year.

In a few cases, the edges of the continents are the boundaries of plates. However, most plate

FIND OUT BY CALCULATING

Traveling Cities

Los Angeles, on the Pacific plate, is slowly moving north-west. San Francisco, on the North American plate, is slowly moving southeast. These two cities are moving toward each other at a rate of about 5 centimeters per year. About 11 million years from now, the two cities will be next to each other. How many meters does each city have to travel before they meet?

Figure 3–8 *This map shows the Earth's most important lithospheric plates. Which plate is most of the United States on? How do the boundaries of the plates relate to the earthquake zones shown in Figure 3–5 on page 61?*

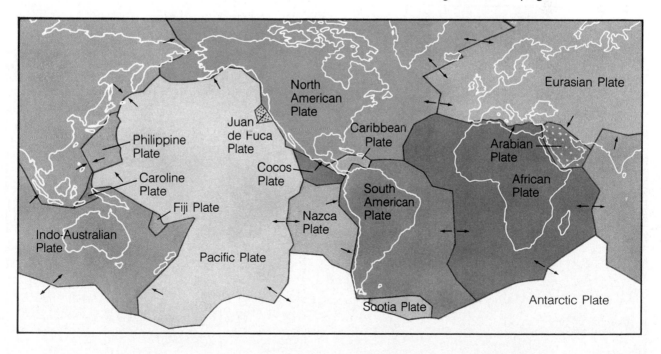

Figure 3–9 *The red areas on this map indicate major volcanic and earthquake sites. These sites also outline the Earth's midocean ridges and trenches. Locate the Ring of Fire on the map.*

boundaries are on the ocean floor. Which two major plates have boundaries at the edges of continents? Where is the boundary between the South American and African plates? What is this boundary called?

Plate Boundaries

There are three types of plate boundaries. The first type occurs at midocean ridges. Because plates move apart (diverge) at midocean ridges, the ridges are called **divergent** (digh-VER-jehnt) **boundaries.** These boundaries are also called constructive boundaries. Why is this an appropriate name?

The second type of plate boundary has trenches. Because the plates come together (converge) at the trenches, the trenches are called **convergent** (kuhn-VER-jehnt) **boundaries.** Why are trenches also called destructive boundaries?

The collision of plates at convergent boundaries causes tremendous pressure and friction. Severe earthquakes often result. As plate material melts in the Earth's mantle, some of it surges upward to produce volcanoes. This explains why the Ring of Fire, a line of volcanoes circling the edge of the Pacific plate, follows the major ocean trenches in that area.

The third type of plate boundary is formed by a lateral fault. Boundaries formed by lateral

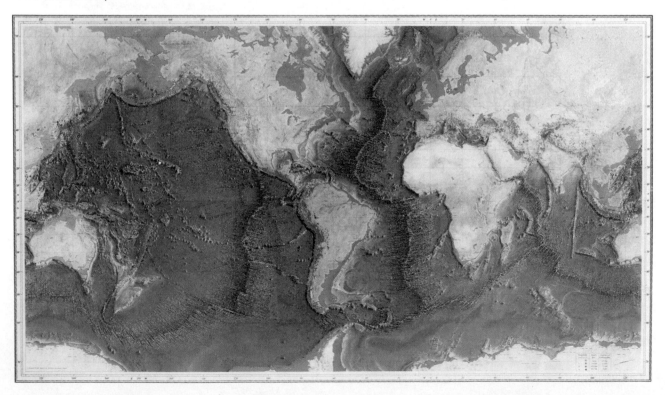

faults are called **strike-slip boundaries.** At a strike-slip boundary, two plates grind together and slip past each other horizontally. No new plate material is made, and no plate material is destroyed. Why do you think a strike-slip boundary is also known as a conservative boundary?

Earthquakes often occur along strike-slip boundaries. An example of a strike-slip boundary is the San Andreas Fault in California. The Pacific plate, on the west, is grinding slowly northwest, while the North American plate is sliding southeast. Today San Francisco is farther north than Los Angeles. But someday Los Angeles, which is on the northward-moving Pacific plate, will be farther north than San Francisco, which is on the North American plate. In about 150 million years, the sliver of California containing Los Angeles will become part of Alaska!

Plate Motion

Scientists are not sure exactly what makes the plates move. They have searched a long time to find the source of the forces that can move continents. One hypothesis is that large **convection currents** within the Earth move the plates.

A convection current is the movement of material caused by differences in temperature. Convection currents move air in the atmosphere and water in the oceans. And they may move the plates of the lithosphere as well. Here's how. Mantle material close to the Earth's core is very hot. Mantle material farther from the core is cooler and denser. The cooler material sinks down toward the Earth's core. The hot material is then pushed up to replace the cooler material. As the cooler material nears the core, it becomes hot and rises once again. The rising and sinking cycle repeats over and over. This type of circular motion carries the plates of the lithosphere along with it, thus causing the continents to move.

Have you ever ridden in a bumper car at an amusement park? If so, you know that it is almost impossible to move without colliding into another bumper car. Like bumper cars, the continents collide with one another as they move. The collision between two continents, however, is far more complex than that between two bumper cars. What happens when continents collide?

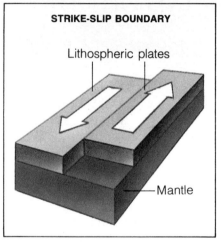

STRIKE-SLIP BOUNDARY

Lithospheric plates

Mantle

Figure 3–10 *At a strike-slip boundary, two plates move past one another horizontally. The San Andreas fault in California is an example of a strike-slip boundary.*

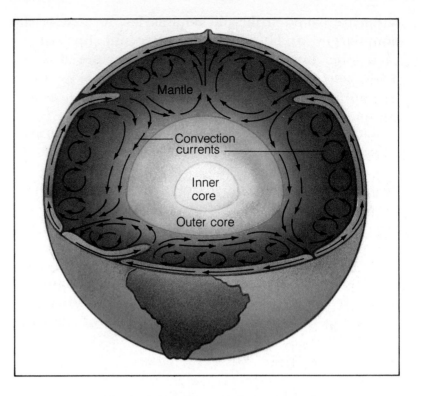

Figure 3–11 *According to one hypothesis, the movement of the lithospheric plates is caused by convection currents. Some supporters of this hypothesis think that the currents run through the entire mantle; others think that only the uppermost part of the mantle is involved.*

Slipping Away

Some scientists hypothe-size that gravity, and not convection currents, is re-sponsible for the movement of the Earth's plates. According to this hypothesis, the plates are tipped upward at their back edge by lava welling up at the midocean rifts, and slide slowly and gradually downward into the trench at their front edge.

You can get an idea of how this process works by floating a dry washcloth in a sink (or bathtub) of water. Watch the edges of the washcloth care-fully. What happens when a washcloth starts to sink? What caused it to start sinking? How does sinking relate to density? What changed the density of the washcloth? What changes the density of a plate?

■ How do your observa-tions relate to the theory of plate tectonics?

When plates converge at trenches, one plate is subducted, or pushed down into the interior of the Earth. How can it be determined which plate will be subducted at a convergent boundary? The answer has to do with the density of the colliding plate edges. The denser plate edge is subducted, and the other plate edge "floats" over it.

When discussing collisions, plates are often de-scribed as oceanic plates or continental plates. An oceanic plate has a colliding edge that consists of dense oceanic crust. A continental plate has a collid-ing edge that contains large amounts of relatively light continental crust. As you read the following descriptions of plate collisions, remember that all plates contain oceanic crust and most plates contain continental crust. Also keep in mind that a lithospheric plate may act as a continental plate in one collision and as an oceanic plate in another.

As you can see in Figure 3–12 on page 70, when an oceanic plate collides with a continental plate, the continental plate rides over the edge of the oceanic plate because the continental plate is less dense. The oceanic plate is subducted into the trench that forms the convergent plate boundary. The subduction of the oceanic plate pushes up and folds the continental crust on the edge of the continental plate. This forms mountain ranges such as the Andes of South America and the northern Cascades of North America. Melting rocks from the oceanic plate rise upward and create volcanoes. Can you explain why there are many active volcanoes along the western edge of South America?

When two oceanic plates collide, the older oceanic plate is subducted under the younger. (Plates grow denser as they cool, and older plates have had longer to cool. Thus older plates are denser.) The plate being subducted melts. Molten rock then rises up and breaks through the surface. As a result, a string of volcanoes erupts on the ocean floor along the trench. In time, this string of undersea volcanoes may rise above the ocean's surface as a string of islands. Because the islands usually appear in a curved line, they are called island arcs. Japan, Indonesia, and the Aleutian Islands are all island arcs.

When two continental plates collide, the edges of the continents fold upward to form large mountain ranges. The Appalachian Mountains of the eastern United States, for example, resulted when Africa collided with North America during the formation of Pangaea. Initially, some of the oceanic crust that lies beneath the continental crust on one of the plates may be subducted. Because continental crust is too light to sink into the Earth, it is scraped off the oceanic crust and piles up at the boundary. But the continental crust cannot pile up forever. Eventually, the boundary jams up and disappears.

In some collisions of continental plates, the plates have approximately the same density. In such collisions, neither plate is subducted, and the edges of the continents thicken greatly and push upward as they are forced together. The Himalayan Mountains formed from such a collision between the Indo-Australian plate and the Eurasian plate. Although the Himalayan Mountains are still being pushed upward, the downward pull of gravity balances their growth and keeps them from getting much higher.

Because Earth's lithospheric plates fit together so closely, any change in one plate or boundary affects all the other plates and boundaries. And there are many changes that can occur in plates and their

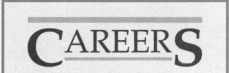

CAREERS

Geophysicist

Scientists who study the processes that change and shape the Earth are called **geophysicists.** Geophysicists study the Earth's surface, interior, oceans, and atmosphere.

People who work in this field attend college and study geology, physics, chemistry, mathematics, and engineering. To learn more about this field, write to the American Geophysical Union, 2000 Florida Ave., NW, Washington, DC 20009.

Figure 3–12 *When an oceanic and a continental plate collide, the oceanic plate is subducted. Some of the material from the melting oceanic plate rises upward and erupts as volcanoes on the continent (top). When two continental plates collide, the continental crust is pushed together and upward to form large mountain ranges (center). When two oceanic plates collide, the denser plate is subducted. Some of the material from the melting plate rises upward and erupts on the ocean floor, forming an island arc (bottom).*

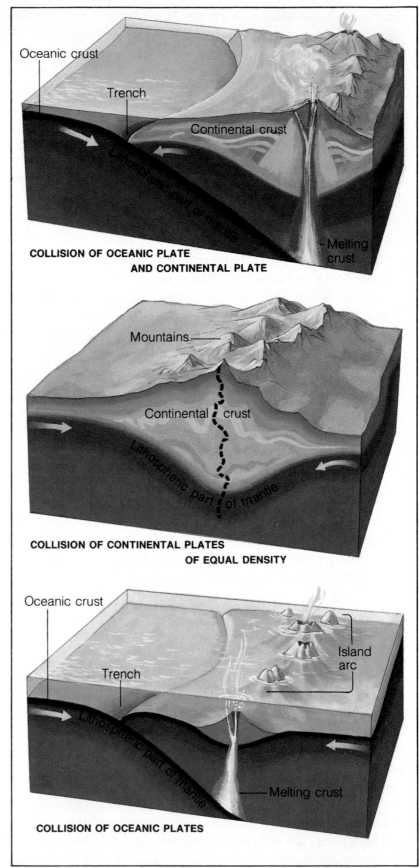

Oceanic crust

Trench

Continental crust

Lithospheric part of mantle

Melting crust

**COLLISION OF OCEANIC PLATE
AND CONTINENTAL PLATE**

Mountains

Continental crust

Lithospheric part of mantle

**COLLISION OF CONTINENTAL PLATES
OF EQUAL DENSITY**

Oceanic crust

Trench

Island arc

Lithospheric part of mantle

Melting crust

COLLISION OF OCEANIC PLATES

FIND OUT BY THINKING

Prefixes

Knowing the meaning of a prefix can often help you re-member the meaning of a word. Using a dictionary, find the meaning of the prefixes *con-*, *di-*, *pan-*, *sub-*, and *trans-*. Relate what you have learned about the prefixes to the definition of the following vocabulary words:

    convection current
    constructive boundary
    Pangaea
    divergent boundary
    subduction
    transform fault

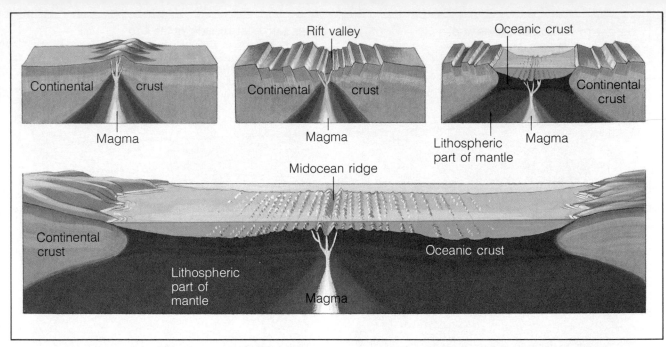

Continental crust

Magma

Rift valley

Continental crust

Magma

Oceanic crust

Continental crust

Lithospheric part of mantle

Magma

Midocean ridge

Continental crust

Lithospheric part of mantle

Magma

Oceanic crust

boundaries. Continental plates may fuse together. A trench may "switch direction" and begin to subduct a formerly overriding plate. New divergent boundaries may form in the center of continents. And plates may be completely subducted and disappear!

The theory of plate tectonics, like Wegener's theory of continental drift, explains how the Earth's surface has changed over time and predicts how it will change in the future. The diagrams in Figure 3–14 on page 72 illustrate what scientists think the Earth has looked like and what it will look like.

Figure 3–13 *New divergent boundaries may form in the center of continents. The formation of the new boundary begins when rising magma heats and weakens an area of a continental plate (top left). The area cracks and sections slip down to form a rift valley (top center). Eventually, ocean water fills in the widening gap between the newly-formed continents. Lava erupting from the rift forms new ocean floor (top right). After millions of years, there is a mature ocean where there was once dry land (bottom).*

3–3 Section Review

1. What is the theory of plate tectonics? How does it relate to continental drift?
2. Describe the three different kinds of plate boundaries.
3. How might convection currents account for the movement of the plates?
4. Explain the origins of volcanoes, earthquakes, and mountains as they relate to plate tectonics.

Connection—*Language Arts*
5. The ocean that surrounded Pangaea is called Panthalassa. The Greek word *thalassa* means sea. Why is the term Panthalassa appropriate? (*Hint:* Look at Figure 3–14.)

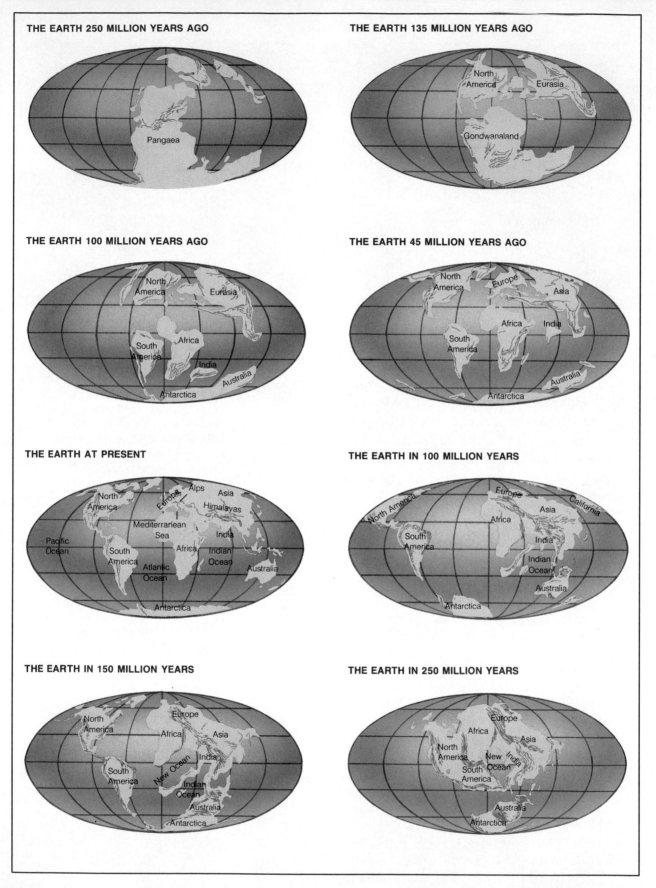

Figure 3–14 *The shapes and positions of Earth's continents have changed greatly.*

CONNECTIONS

Plate Tectonics and Life on Earth

The *evolution of Earth's living things* is strongly linked to the movements of the lithospheric plates. Why? Because living things evolve in response to changes in their environment. And the movement of the plates causes changes in climate, in geographic features such as mountains, and in the types of living things with which a species (specific type of living thing) interacts.

When the history of the Earth and its living things is studied, some basic patterns occur over and over again. One pattern is that when landmasses join together, diversity decreases. For example, fossils indicate that there were once 29 families of mammals in South America and 27 entirely different families of mammals in North America. (A family is a scientific group containing many related kinds of animals. The cat family, for example, includes lions, tigers, and house cats.) Soon after the continents joined together—about 3 million years ago—there were only 22 families left. Only the families that competed the most successfully survived; the rest died out.

Yet another pattern is that when landmasses split apart, the diversity of land animals increases. On a big landmass, animals can easily move to suitable places and avoid the more challenging environments. On a small landmass, animals are stuck where they are and thus must adapt to local conditions. At the same time, the animals are cut off from competitors and natural enemies on other landmasses. This combination of conditions results in the development of an enormous number of new species.

The world's monkeys and apes are one example of diversity caused by the breakup of a landmass. The splitting up of South America and Africa roughly 45 million years ago resulted in monkeys evolving into two distinct groups. New World monkeys are primarily tree-dwellers that have long tails used for grasping and for balance. Although Old World monkeys include tree-dwellers as well as ground-dwellers, none has a grasping tail.

Laboratory Investigation

Mapping Lithospheric Plates

Problem

How are the locations of the Earth's volcanoes, earthquakes, and mountain ranges related to the locations of the lithospheric plates?

Materials *(per student)*

> colored pencils (black, red, brown, green)
>
> paper   chapter maps

Procedure

1. With the black pencil, trace the outline of the world map onto the paper.

2. Draw with a red pencil the Ring of Fire on the world map. Also draw the other earthquake and volcano zones.

3. Shade in the general boundaries of the world's mountain ranges with a brown pencil. Be sure to include the Himalayas, Alps, Andes, and Rockies.

4. Draw in with a green pencil the boundaries of the seven lithospheric plates as well as the boundaries of the Arabian and Caribbean plates. Label each plate.

Observations

1. What is the relationship of the Ring of Fire to the Pacific plate?

2. Where are the most earthquakes, volcanoes, and mountains located in relation to the lithospheric plates?

Analysis and Conclusions

1. From the map you have made and the information in this chapter, how can you explain the apparent relationships between the lithospheric plates and the occurrence of earthquakes, volcanoes, and mountain ranges?

2. **On Your Own** Some volcanic activity is due to "hot spots." Using references from the library, find out what hot spots are and where the major hot spots are located. Using a blue pencil, mark the locations of the major hot spots on your map. Explain how hot spots provide evidence for plate movement.

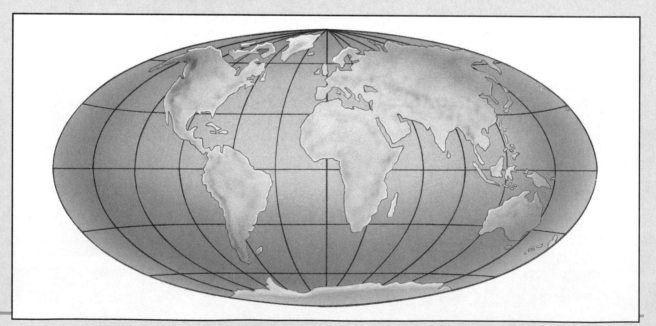

Study Guide

Summarizing Key Concepts

3–1 Earth's Drifting Continents

▲ The theory of continental drift, formulated by Alfred Wegener, states that all the continents were once part of one giant landmass, Pangaea. Pangaea split apart, and the continents slowly moved to their present positions.

▲ Wegener's theory is based on evidence from fossils and rock formations.

▲ The location of the Earth's landmasses affects their climate.

3–2 Earth's Spreading Ocean Floor

▲ Ocean-floor spreading occurs as parts of the ocean floor move away from a rift valley in the center of a midocean ridge. New ocean floor forms as molten rock rises through the rift and hardens.

▲ Ocean floor is destroyed when it is subducted into trenches and melted inside the mantle.

▲ The ocean floor is made of pieces that move from rifts to trenches. Many of these moving pieces have continents on top of them.

▲ Both the ages of the ocean-floor rocks and the magnetic stripes on the ocean floor are evidence of ocean-floor spreading.

3–3 Earth's Moving Plates

▲ The theory of plate tectonics, which links together the ideas of continental drift and ocean-floor spreading, explains how the Earth has evolved over time. It helps to explain the formation and destruction of the Earth's crust and its movements and collisions.

▲ The lithosphere, which consists of the crust and a thick layer of relatively cool, rigid mantle rock, is made of a number of plates.

▲ Plates usually contain both oceanic and continental crust.

▲ Divergent plate boundaries are formed by the midocean ridges.

▲ Convergent plate boundaries are formed by the trenches.

▲ Strike-slip boundaries are formed by lateral faults at which two plates slide horizontally past each other.

▲ Some scientists hypothesize that plate movement is caused by convection currents within the mantle.

▲ Understanding how the plates have moved in the past makes it possible to predict their future movement.

Reviewing Key Terms

Define each term in a complete sentence.

3–1 Earth's Drifting Continents
fossil
Pangaea
theory of continental drift

3–2 Earth's Spreading Ocean Floor
midocean ridge
ocean-floor spreading
transform fault
trench
subduction

3–3 Earth's Moving Plates
theory of plate tectonics
plate
tectonics
lithosphere
divergent boundary
convergent boundary
strike-slip boundary
convection current

Chapter Review

Content Review

Multiple Choice

Choose the letter of the answer that best completes each statement.

1. Alfred Wegener is most closely associated with the theory of
   a. the contracting Earth.
   b. continental drift.
   c. plate tectonics.
   d. ocean-floor spreading.
2. A deep crack that runs through the center of a midocean ridge is called a
   a. trench.   c. lithosphere.
   b. rift valley.   d. transform fault.
3. The collision of two oceanic plates creates
   a. mountain belts.   c. rift valleys.
   b. convection currents.   d. island arcs.
4. Evidence that supports the theory of continental drift has been provided by
   a. coal fields.   c. fossils.
   b. glacial deposits.   d. all of these.

5. The movement of the ocean floor on either side of a midocean ridge is best known as
   a. rifting.   c. ocean-floor spreading.
   b. glaciation.   d. subduction.
6. Plates containing crust and upper mantle form the Earth's
   a. lithosphere.   c. core.
   b. hydrosphere.   d. atmosphere.
7. The process in which the ocean floor plunges into the Earth's interior is called
   a. construction.   c. rifting.
   b. subduction.   d. convection.
8. Two plates grind past each other at a
   a. constructive boundary.
   b. divergent boundary.
   c. convergent boundary.
   d. strike-slip boundary.

True or False

If the statement is true, write "true." If it is false, change the underlined word or words to make the statement true.

1. The largest lithospheric plate is the Pacific.
2. Wegener proposed that all the continents were once part of one large landmass called Gondwanaland.
3. Ocean floor is subducted at transform boundaries.
4. Conduction currents may be the cause of plate movement.
5. Midocean rifts are also known as convergent, or destructive, boundaries.
6. Magnetic stripes on the ocean floor indicate that the Earth's magnetic poles reverse themselves from time to time.

Concept Mapping

Complete the following concept map for Section 3–1. Refer to pages J6–J7 to construct a concept map for the entire chapter.

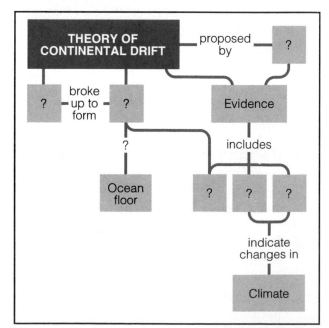

Concept Mastery

Discuss each of the following in a brief paragraph.

1. How do plate movements relate to volcanoes and earthquakes?
2. What kinds of evidence are used to support the theory of continental drift?
3. Describe what happens in the three different kinds of plate collisions.
4. What is a lithospheric plate?
5. How might convection currents account for the movement of the continents?
6. What is ocean-floor spreading? How does it relate to the theories of continental drift and plate tectonics?
7. How are the magnetic stripes on the ocean floor formed? Why are these stripes significant?
8. How does plate tectonics explain the formation of mountains?

Critical Thinking and Problem Solving

Use the skills you have developed in this chapter to answer each of the following.

1. **Making comparisons** How are the theories of continental drift and plate tectonics similar? How are they different?
2. **Developing a hypothesis** Studies have shown that continents appear to consist of small pieces that come from many different parts of the Earth. Using what you know about plate tectonics and isostasy, develop a hypothesis to explain how Earth's "crazy quilt" continents were formed.
3. **Analyzing data** The two imaginary continents in the accompanying figure each have three rock sections. The arrows show the magnetic field direction that existed when each section formed. The rocks' ages are shown in billions of years. Reptile fossils are found in sections A, B, and Z; fish fossils in sections C and X.
   On a piece of paper, trace all the information given in the figure. Cut out both continents. Then follow the instructions and answer the questions.
   a. Try to fit the two continents together. Do they fit more than one way? Choose the better fit. Explain what evidence you used to make your choice.
   b. What is your best estimate of the age of the rocks in section Z?

4. **Evaluating theories** Mountains almost always appear as long, narrow, curving ranges located at the edges of continents. Mountain ranges vary greatly in age. Most scientists once thought that mountains formed because the Earth was contracting. This caused the surface to wrinkle up like a raisin. If the contraction hypothesis were correct, what would you expect to be true about the age and distribution of mountains? Explain why the theory of continental drift better accounts for the age and distribution of mountains.
5. **Using the writing process** Write a humorous, but accurate, skit in which Alfred Wegener and one of his opponents appear on a major daytime talk show.

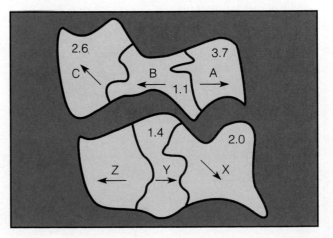

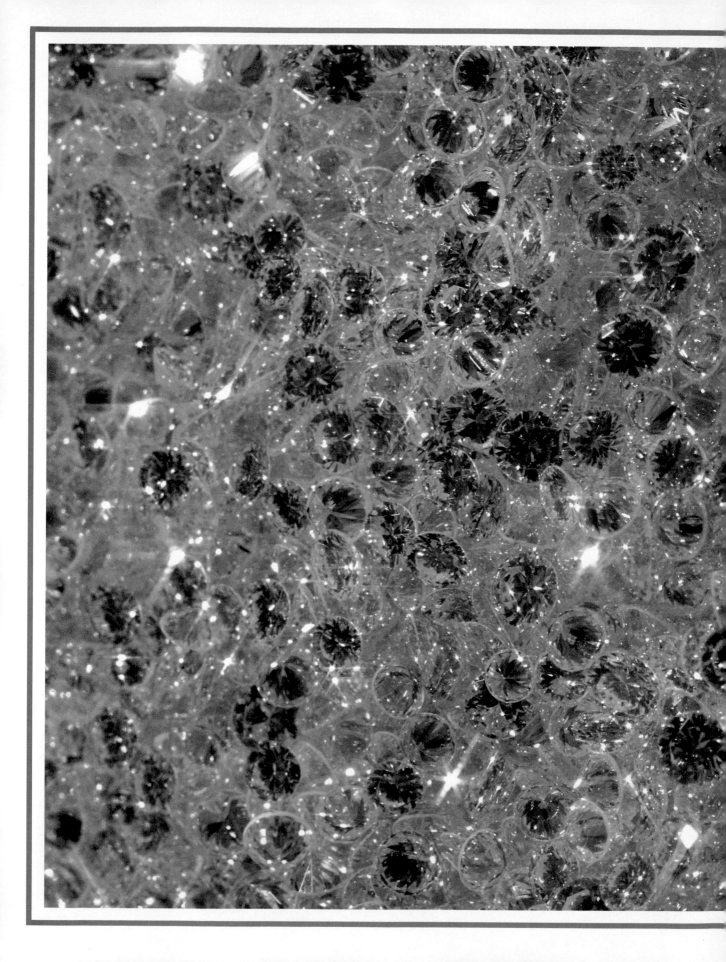

Rocks and Minerals

Guide for Reading

After you read the following sections, you will be able to

4–1 What Is a Mineral?

- Define the term mineral.

4–2 Uses of Minerals

- Differentiate among metals, nonmetals, ores, and gemstones.

4–3 What Is a Rock?

- Describe the rock cycle.

4–4 Fluid and Fire: Igneous Rocks

- Explain how igneous rocks are classified.

4–5 Slowly Built Layers: Sedimentary Rocks

- Identify the main categories of sedimentary rocks.

4–6 Changes in Form: Metamorphic Rocks

- Describe the forces that change existing rocks into metamorphic rocks.

For hundreds of years, diamonds have been prized as a symbol of great wealth and power. Many of the world's largest diamonds adorn the scepters and crowns of kings and queens and decorate the jewelry of the extremely wealthy.

Some of the largest and most precious diamonds have dramatic histories. For example, the large, dark-blue gem now known as the Hope diamond is said to have once been an eye in the statue of an Indian goddess. When the diamond was stolen, the goddess is said to have cursed the stone and decreed that it would bring bad luck to all those who wore it. The diamond was owned and worn by King Louis XVI of France and his queen, both of whom were later beheaded during the French Revolution. Soon after the revolution, the diamond disappeared. When it reappeared nearly forty years later, it continued to be linked with murders, tragic accidents, and other misfortunes as it passed from owner to owner in Europe and the United States. The Hope diamond now rests in a display case at the Smithsonian Institution in Washington, DC.

Diamonds and other gemstones—rubies, emeralds, and sapphires, to name a few—are types of minerals. Minerals are the building blocks of rocks, and rocks are the building blocks of the solid Earth. Read on, and learn more about rocks and minerals.

Journal *Activity*

You and Your World You can probably think of many ways in which rocks have affected your life. In your journal, describe an incident in your life in which a rock played an important part.

◀ *Diamond is one of the most beautiful and precious of Earth's minerals.*

4–1 What Is a Mineral?

Animal, vegetable, or mineral?

If you have ever played the guessing game Twenty Questions, this phrase should be familiar to you. In the game, the word **mineral** refers to anything that is not living. In science, however, the word mineral has a more specific meaning. **A mineral is a naturally occurring, inorganic solid that has a definite chemical composition and crystal structure.** In order for a substance to be called a mineral, it must have all five of the characteristics described in this definition. Let's look at each characteristic more closely.

A mineral must occur naturally in the Earth. Silver, asbestos, and talc (the main ingredient of talcum powder), which all occur naturally, are minerals. Steel and cement, which are manufactured substances, are not minerals.

A mineral must be **inorganic,** or not formed from living things or the remains of living things. Quartz, which makes up about 11 percent of the Earth's crust, is a mineral. Coal and oil, although found in naturally occurring underground deposits, are not minerals because they are formed from the remains of living things that existed long ago.

A mineral is always a solid. Like all solids, a mineral has a definite volume and shape. Can you explain why oxygen, which occurs naturally and is inorganic, is not a mineral?

A mineral has a definite chemical composition. A mineral may be made of a single pure substance, or element, such as gold, copper, or sulfur. The minerals diamond and graphite (the main ingredient in pencil lead) are both made of the element carbon. Most minerals, however, are made of two or more elements chemically combined to form a compound.

A mineral's atoms are arranged in a definite pattern repeated over and over again. Atoms are the building blocks of matter. If not confined, the repeating pattern of a mineral's atoms forms a solid called a **crystal.** A crystal has flat sides that

Figure 4–1 *The calcite crystals, fossil-bearing limestone, and pearls are all made of the compound calcium carbonate. Yet only the calcite is considered to be a mineral. Why?*

Figure 4–2 *Minerals have a definite chemical composition. Some, such as copper (left) and sulfur (bottom right), contain only one kind of element. Others are made up of compounds. Covellite (top right) is made up of a compound that contains copper and sulfur atoms.*

meet in sharp edges and corners. All minerals have a characteristic crystal shape.

There are about 2500 different kinds of minerals. Some minerals are very common and easy to find. Others are rare and valuable. But all minerals have the five characteristics you have just read about.

Formation and Composition of Minerals

Many minerals come from magma, the molten rock beneath the Earth's surface. When magma cools, mineral crystals are formed. How magma cools and where it cools determine the size of the mineral crystals.

When magma cools slowly beneath the Earth's crust, large crystals form. When magma cools rapidly beneath the Earth's crust, small crystals form. Sometimes the molten rock reaches the surface of the Earth and cools so quickly that no crystals at all form.

Crystals may also form from compounds dissolved in a liquid such as water. When the liquid evaporates, or changes to a gas, it leaves behind the minerals as crystals. The size of the crystals depends on the speed of evaporation. If evaporation is slow, larger crystals will form. The minerals halite, or rock salt, and calcite form in this way.

FIND OUT BY
DOING

Rock-Forming Minerals

1. Collect between five and ten different kinds of rocks from your neighborhood.

2. Use a rock and mineral field guide to identify the minerals that make up each rock you found.

■ What minerals were found in your rocks?

■ What are the most common rock-forming minerals?

Figure 4–3 *These richly-colored emerald crystals formed as magma slowly cooled deep inside the Earth (left). The delicate clusters of gypsum crystals known as desert roses are formed by evaporation (right).*

As you can see in Figure 4–4, the elements oxygen and silicon make up almost 75 percent of the Earth's crust. Other elements found in large amounts in the Earth's crust are aluminum, iron, calcium, sodium, potassium, and magnesium. Since these 8 elements are the most abundant elements in the Earth's crust, most common minerals are made of combinations of these elements.

There are about 100 common minerals formed from the 8 most abundant elements. Of these 100 common minerals, fewer than 20 are widely distributed in the Earth's crust. These minerals make up almost all the rocks in the crust. Scientists call these minerals rock-forming minerals. Quartz, calcite, augite, hematite, micas, and feldspars are examples of rock-forming minerals.

Identifying Minerals

Because there are so many different kinds of minerals, it is not an easy task to tell them apart. In fact, it is usually difficult to identify a mineral simply by looking at it. For example, the three minerals in Figure 4–5 all look like gold. Yet only one actually is gold.

Minerals have certain physical properties that can be used to identify them. Some of these properties can be seen just by looking at a mineral. Other properties can be observed only through special tests. By learning how to recognize the properties of minerals, you will be able to more easily identify many common minerals around you.

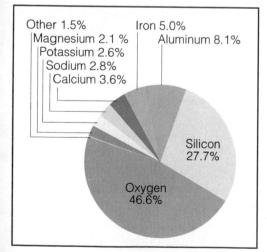

Figure 4–4 *Eight elements make up more than 98 percent of the Earth's crust. Which element accounts for nearly 50 percent?*

Figure 4–5 *All that glitters is not always gold. The delicate branches among the quartz crystals are the real thing (left). The imitators are chalcopyrite (center) and pyrite (right). Can you explain why pyrite is also known as "fool's gold"?*

COLOR The color of a mineral is an easily observed physical property. But color can be used to identify only those few minerals that always have their own characteristic color. The mineral malachite is always green. The mineral azurite is always blue. No other minerals look quite the same as these.

Many minerals, however, come in a variety of colors. The mineral quartz is usually colorless. But it may be yellow, brown, black, green, pink, or purple. (The gemstone amethyst is purple quartz.) As you can see in Figure 4–6, color alone cannot be used to identify quartz and other minerals that have many different forms.

Color is not always a reliable way to identify minerals for another reason. The colors of minerals can change as a result of exposure to or treatment with heat, cold, pollution, or radiation.

Figure 4–6 *The color of lemon-yellow mimetite (right) and red-orange crocoite (center) may be their most obvious physical property. But color alone cannot be used to identify minerals. Some minerals are similar in color. Other minerals, such as quartz, come in many different colors (left).*

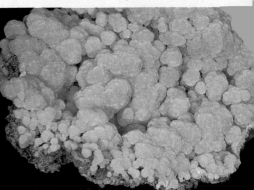

LUSTER The **luster** of a mineral describes the way a mineral reflects light from its surface. Certain minerals reflect light the way highly polished metal does. Such minerals—including silver, copper, gold, pyrite, and graphite—have a metallic luster.

Minerals that do not reflect much light have a nonmetallic luster. Nonmetallic lusters may be described by a number of different terms: brilliant, glassy, pearly, silky, and dull, to name a few.

HARDNESS The ability of a mineral to resist being scratched is known as its **hardness.** Hardness is one of the most useful properties for identifying minerals. Friedrich Mohs, a German mineralogist, worked out a scale of hardness for minerals. He used ten minerals and arranged them in order of increasing hardness. The number 1 is assigned to the softest mineral, talc. Diamond, the hardest of the ten minerals, is given the number 10. Each mineral will scratch any mineral with a lower number and will be scratched by any mineral with a higher number. Figure 4–8 shows the minerals of the Mohs hardness scale with their assigned numbers. What mineral is harder than talc but softer than calcite? What minerals would you expect quartz to scratch?

Figure 4–7 *Because quartz reflects light like glass, it is said to have a glassy luster. Diamond has a brilliant luster. Talc's luster ranges from pearly to greasy. And malachite's luster ranges from glassy to silky. Which end of this range is shown by the malachite in the photograph?*

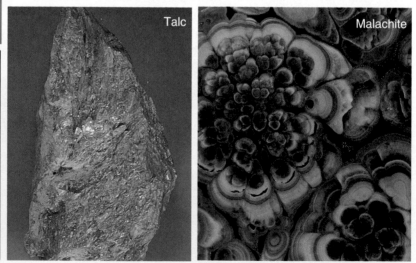

To determine the hardness of an unknown mineral, the mineral is rubbed against the surface of each mineral in the hardness scale. If the unknown mineral is scratched by the known mineral, it is softer than the known mineral. If the unknown mineral scratches the known mineral, it is harder than that mineral. If two minerals do not scratch each other, they have the same hardness. What is the hardness of a mineral sample that scratches quartz and is scratched by corundum but not by topaz?

STREAK The color of the powder scraped off a mineral when it is rubbed against a hard, rough surface is called its **streak.** Streak can be an excellent clue to identifying some minerals. Even though the color of a mineral may vary, its streak is always the same. This streak, however, may be different from the color of the mineral itself. For example, hematite may be gray, green, or black, but it always has a reddish-brown streak.

Streak can be observed by rubbing the mineral sample across a piece of unglazed porcelain, which is called a streak plate. The back of a piece of bathroom tile makes an excellent streak plate. A streak

MOHS HARDNESS SCALE

Mineral	Hardness
Talc	1
Gypsum	2
Calcite	3
Fluorite	4
Apatite	5
Feldspars	6
Quartz	7
Topaz	8
Corundum	9
Diamond	10

Figure 4–8 *The Mohs hardness scale is a list of ten minerals that represent different degrees of hardness. As you might expect, quartz is about 7 times as hard as talc, and corundum (the mineral of which rubies and sapphires are made) is about 9 times as hard as talc. Diamond, however, is about 40 times (not 10 times) as hard as talc. Diamonds are extremely hard!*

FIELD HARDNESS SCALE

Hardness	Common Tests
1	Easily scratched with a fingernail (2.5)
2	Scratched by fingernail
3	Very easily scratched by a knife (5.5–6); will not scratch a copper penny (3)
4	Easily scratched by a knife
5	Difficult to scratch with a knife; will not scratch glass (5.5–6)
6	Scratched by a steel file (6.5–7); may barely scratch glass
7	May barely scratch a steel file; easily scratches glass
8–10	Scratches a steel file

Figure 4–9 *A field hardness scale can be used when the minerals from the Mohs scale are not available. What is a disadvantage of using a field scale rather than the Mohs scale?*

How Hard Could It Be?

Obtain a penny, a penknife, a piece of glass, a steel file, and at least five different mineral samples.

■ What is the approximate hardness of each of your mineral samples?

plate has a hardness slightly less than 7. Can you explain why a streak test cannot be done on a mineral whose hardness is greater than 7?

Many minerals have white or colorless streaks. Talc, gypsum, and quartz are examples. Streak is not a useful physical property in identifying minerals such as these.

DENSITY Every mineral has a property called **density.** Density is the amount of matter in a given space. Density can also be expressed as mass per unit volume. The density of a mineral is always the same, no matter what the size of the mineral sample. Because each mineral has a characteristic density, one mineral can easily be compared with any other mineral. You can compare the densities of two minerals of about the same size by picking them up and hefting them. The denser mineral feels heavier.

CRYSTAL SHAPE As you have already learned, minerals have a characteristic crystal shape that results from the way the atoms or molecules come together as the mineral is forming. As you can see in Figure 4–10, there are six basic shapes of crystals, or crystal systems.

CLEAVAGE AND FRACTURE The terms **cleavage** and **fracture** are used to describe the way a mineral breaks. Cleavage is the tendency of a mineral to split along smooth, definite surfaces. Some minerals

Figure 4–10 *The six basic crystal systems are shown here. The dashed lines on the crystal diagrams represent special lines called axes (AK-seez). The length and position of the axes relative to one another determine the system to which a crystal belongs.*

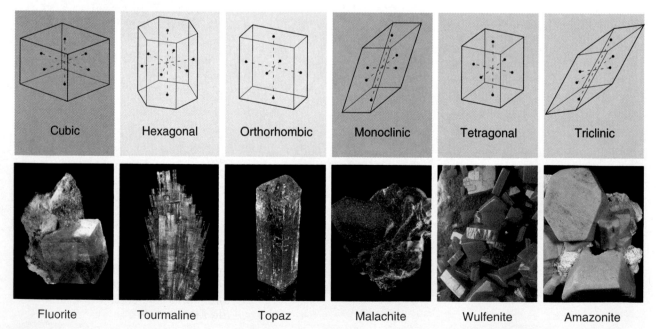

Cubic	Hexagonal	Orthorhombic	Monoclinic	Tetragonal	Triclinic
Fluorite	Tourmaline	Topaz	Malachite	Wulfenite	Amazonite

cleave quite well. Halite, for example, always cleaves in three directions, breaking into small cubes. Micas cleave along one surface, making layer after layer of very thin sheets.

Most minerals, however, do not break along smooth, definite surfaces. Instead, they break along rough or jagged surfaces. This type of break is known as fracture. Like cleavage, fracture is a property that helps to identify a mineral. For example, quartz has a shell-shaped fracture that has a number of smooth, curved surfaces and that resembles chipped glass.

SPECIAL PROPERTIES Some minerals can be identified by special properties. Magnetite is naturally magnetic. Fluorite glows when put under ultraviolet light. Halite tastes salty. Sulfur smells like rotten eggs or burning rubber. Calcite fizzes when hydrochloric acid is added to it. And uraninite (one of the sources of uranium) is radioactive.

Figure 4–11 *The way a mineral breaks is a clue to its identity. Mica cleaves into thin sheets (left). Calcite cleaves into shapes resembling slanted boxes (center). Quartz has a shell-shaped fracture. The broken surface has curved ridges like those on a clam's shell (right).*

4–1 Section Review

1. Define the term mineral. Briefly describe the five characteristics of minerals.
2. What kinds of physical properties are used to identify minerals?
3. How is a mineral's hardness tested?
4. What is the difference between cleavage and fracture?

Critical Thinking—*Applying Concepts*
5. How would you go about determining if a yellow pebble is a valuable topaz or a not-so-valuable citrine (yellow quartz)? What would you do differently if you needed to identify a cut and polished gem without damaging it? Explain.

Figure 4–12 *Under ordinary light, calcite and willemite look quite plain. But under ultraviolet light, these minerals glow with unexpected colors.*

4–2 Uses of Minerals

Throughout history, people have used minerals. At first, minerals were used just as they came from the Earth. Later, people learned to combine and process the Earth's minerals. **Today many of the Earth's minerals are used to meet the everyday needs of people.** Minerals are raw materials for a wide variety of products from dyes to dishes and from table salt to televisions.

Ores

The term **ores** is used to describe minerals or combinations of minerals from which metals and nonmetals can be removed in usable amounts. **Metals** are elements that have shiny surfaces and are able to conduct electricity and heat. Metals can be hammered or pressed into thin sheets and other shapes without breaking. Metals can also be pulled into thin strands without breaking. Iron, lead, aluminum, copper, silver, and gold are examples of metals.

Most metals are found combined with other substances in ores. So after the ores are removed from the Earth by mining, the metals must be removed from the ores. During a process called smelting, an ore is heated in such a way that the metal can be

Figure 4–13 *Chrysocolla is an ore of the metal copper. Copper is used in electrical wire. What are some other uses of copper?*

separated from it. For example, iron is obtained from ores such as limonite and hematite. Lead can be processed from the ore galena. Aluminum comes from the ore bauxite.

Metals are very useful. Iron is used in making steel. Copper is used in pipes and electrical wire. Aluminum is used in the production of cans, foil, lightweight motors, and airplanes. Silver and gold are used in dental fillings and in decorative objects such as jewelry. Pure metals may be combined to form other metallic substances. For example, lead and tin are melted together to make pewter, which is used to make bowls, platters, and decorative objects. Chromium and iron are melted together to make stainless steel. And copper and zinc are combined to make brass.

Nonmetals are elements that have dull surfaces and are poor conductors of electricity and heat. Nonmetals are not easily shaped. Sulfur and halite are examples of nonmetals.

Some nonmetals are removed from the Earth in usable form. Other nonmetals must be processed to separate them from the ores in which they are found.

Like metals, nonmetals are quite useful. Sulfur is one of the most useful nonmetals. It is used to make matches, medicines, and fertilizers. It is also used in iron and steel production.

FIND OUT BY READING

Neither a Borrower Nor a Lender Be

Because of their beauty and value, gems can have a powerful effect on people. Sometimes they can even change a person's life. Read the short story *The Necklace* by Guy de Maupassant.

Figure 4–14 *Red-orange cinnabar is the main ore of mercury, a metal often used in thermometers. Purple fluorite is the main ore of the nonmetal fluorine. Fluorine compounds have many different uses—you probably use the fluorine compounds known as fluorides every time you brush your teeth!*

Figure 4–15 *Some minerals, such as beryl (left), topaz (center), and garnet (right), are considered gemstones. What are gemstones?*

Gemstones

Some minerals are hard, beautiful, and durable substances that can be cut and polished for jewelry and decoration. Such minerals are called **gemstones.** Once a gemstone is cut and polished, it is called a gem. The rarest and most valuable gemstones—diamonds, rubies, sapphires, and emeralds—are known as precious stones. All other gemstones are known as semiprecious stones. Amethysts, zircons, garnets, turquoises, and tourmalines are just a few examples of semiprecious stones. They are all beautiful and durable, but they are not as rare and as valuable as precious stones.

Although many gems are minerals, there are a few that are not. Pearls, which are produced by oysters and mussels, and amber, which is fossilized tree sap, are gemstones. But they are not minerals. Can you explain why?

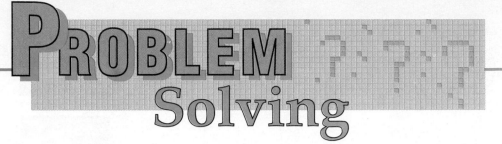
A Gem of a Puzzle

Imagine the following situation. Hearing that you have gotten pretty good at identifying minerals, a wealthy (and rather eccentric) gem dealer has challenged you to identify three beautifully cut gems. If you can correctly identify the gems, you get to keep them.

As you can see in the accompanying figure, the gem dealer has presented you with the three gems, a table of information, and five vials containing thick, rather smelly liquids.

Applying Concepts

1. Describe the procedure you plan to use to identify the gems.

2. What results would you expect to obtain for sapphire (corundum)? For quartz?

3. Suppose that one of the gems sinks slowly in solution C, floats on the top of solution E, and stays at whatever depth you put it in solution D. What mineral is this gem made of?

4. Explain how you can tell the difference between cubic zirconia and zircon using only the materials available to you. (It can be done.)

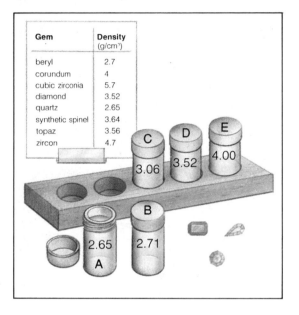

Gem	Density (g/cm³)
beryl	2.7
corundum	4
cubic zirconia	5.7
diamond	3.52
quartz	2.65
synthetic spinel	3.64
topaz	3.56
zircon	4.7

4–2 Section Review

1. Describe five different ways in which minerals are used.
2. What is an ore? Why are ores smelted?
3. How do metals differ from nonmetals?
4. List three examples each of precious and semi-precious stones.

Connection—*Economics*
5. If the demand for an object exceeds the supply, the price of the object will go up. In general, rubies and emeralds are far more expensive than diamonds. What can you infer from this?

Genuine Imitations

In the past hundred years or so, advances in *chemical technology* have made it possible to create crystals that have the same structure, composition, and appearance as natural minerals do. These synthetic (made by humans) gemstones are produced by a number of different processes and have a variety of different uses.

As you might expect, many synthetic gemstones are used for jewelry. But you might be surprised to know that most synthetic sapphires and rubies are used for more practical purposes. Fine mechanical watches have parts that are made of tiny pieces of synthetic ruby. (This is why such watches advertise that they have 17-jewel or 21-jewel movements.) The microcircuits, or chips, used in aircraft, satellites, and nuclear reactors are formed on a base of synthetic sapphire. Lasers, compasses, electric meters, quartz watches, and cloth-making machines are among the many devices that also contain parts made from synthetic rubies and sapphires. Even the glass plate in most supermarket scanners is coated with synthetic sapphire.

It is quite possible that supermarket scanners and many other objects will one day have a more scratch-resistant coating than sapphire. That coating will be made of synthetic diamond. Watch crystals, scanner windows, and stereo speakers with diamond coatings are being commercially manufactured already. Experts predict that diamond-coated razor blades, computer hard disks, drill bits, and pots and pans may be available in the not-so-distant future.

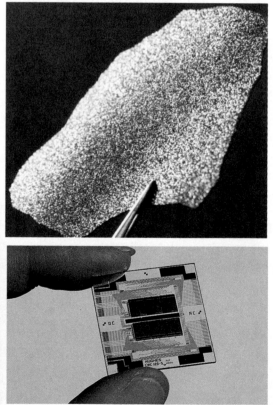

4–3 What Is a Rock?

Rocks are probably a familiar sight to you. You see them all around you in various shapes, sizes, and colors. Rocks are the building blocks of the Earth. They form beaches, mountains, the ocean floor, and all the other parts of the Earth's crust.

Humans have been using rocks for a long time. About 2 million years ago, ancestors of modern humans shaped small pieces of rocks into stone tools and weapons. Stonehenge in Great Britain, the Great Pyramid of Egypt, the Great Wall of China, the city of Machu Pichu in Peru, and the city of Great Zimbabwe in southern Africa were all built of rocks hundreds of years ago. What are some other ways in which humans used rocks in the past? How do they use rocks today?

It is easy to tell that something is made from rocks. It is also easy to recognize a rock when you see one. But what exactly is a rock?

In science, a rock is a hard substance composed of one or more minerals. Usually, a rock is made of more than one kind of mineral. Recall that the most common minerals in rocks are made of the elements that are most abundant in the Earth's crust. What are the eight most abundant elements in the crust?

A rock may also be made of or contain naturally occurring substances that do not perfectly fit the definition of a mineral. For example, rocks may be composed of volcanic glass or of opal. Both these substances lack a crystalline structure and so are not minerals in the strictest sense of the word.

Types of Rocks

To make sense of the enormous diversity of rocks in the world, it is necessary to organize them in a logical way. Geologists (people who study the structure and history of the Earth) place rocks into groups based on certain characteristics. **Rocks are placed into three groups according to how they form: igneous, sedimentary, and metamorphic.**

Igneous (IHG-nee-uhs) rocks were originally hot, fluid magma within the Earth. Igneous rocks get their name from the Latin word *ignis,* which means

Guide for Reading

Focus on these questions as you read.
▶ How are rocks classified?
▶ What is the rock cycle?

Figure 4–16 *The Aztecs, who lived long ago in what is now Mexico, created magnificent buildings and works of art out of rocks.*

Figure 4–17 *Igneous rocks are formed when molten rock cools and hardens. Red-hot lava still glows beneath a crust of basalt in this fresh lava flow in Hawaii (left). Sedimentary rocks may be formed as layer upon layer of particles build up on the bottom of a sea. These layers may be revealed as plate movements drain seas and raise the rocks that once rested on the ocean floor (center). Metamorphic rocks form when heat, pressure, and chemical reactions change existing rock into something new. The process of change may cause the minerals within the rock to separate into layers, forming distinct bands (right).*

fire. Do you think that igneous rock is an appropriate name?

Most **sedimentary** (sehd-ih-MEHN-tuh-ree) rocks are formed from particles that have been carried along and deposited by wind and water. These particles, or **sediments** (SEHD-ih-mehnts), include bits of rock in the form of mud, sand, or pebbles. Sediments also include shells, bones, leaves, stems, and other remains of living things. Over time, these particles become pressed or cemented together to form rocks.

Metamorphic (meht-ah-MOR-fihk) rocks are formed when chemical reactions, tremendous heat, and/or great pressure change existing rocks into new kinds of rocks. These new rocks (metamorphic rocks) have physical and chemical properties that are usually quite different from the original rocks. The root word *morph* means form, and the prefix *meta-* means change. Why is the term metamorphic an appropriate one?

The Rock Cycle

In the previous three chapters, you learned that the Earth's surface is not at all as permanent and unchanging as it sometimes seems to be. Mountains fault and fold upward; volcanoes build new islands in the ocean; tectonic plates move. The rocks that form the Earth's surface are also subject to change. Igneous and sedimentary rocks may be transformed by heat, pressure, or chemical reactions into metamorphic rocks. Metamorphic rocks may change into other kinds of metamorphic rocks. Metamorphic rocks may be remelted and become igneous rocks again. The continuous changing of rocks from one kind to another over long periods of time is called the **rock cycle.**

Many cycles exist in nature. Some of these cycles, such as the phases of the moon or the seasons of the year, occur in a definite sequence. For example, the sequence of the seasons is winter, spring, summer, and autumn. In contrast, the rock cycle has no definite sequence. It can follow many different pathways. Look at Figure 4–18. The outer circle shows the complete rock cycle. The arrows within the circle show alternate pathways that can be taken, and often are.

Let's follow the material in a rock on its long journey through the rock cycle. In the right-hand photograph in Figure 4–18, a huge dome of granite, an igneous rock, lies exposed to the wind and rain, the cold of winter, and the heat of summer.

Because granite is made of hard minerals such as quartz and feldspars, it is quite resistant to nature's

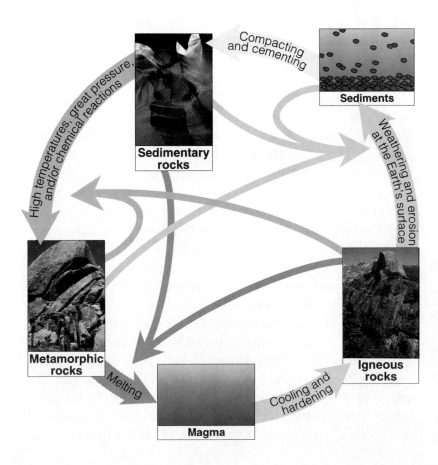

Figure 4–18 *The photographs that illustrate this diagram of the rock cycle show Half Dome, a granite formation in Yosemite National Park, California (right); sandstone in Antelope Canyon, Arizona (top); and a quartzite formation in Joshua Tree National Monument, California (left). What kind of rock does each of these photographs represent? How does rock change from one type to another?*

Figure 4–19 *The changing seasons form a cycle in nature in which events always happen in the same order. How does this cycle differ from the rock cycle?*

FIND OUT BY WRITING

Famous Rock Formations

Using reference materials in the library, find out more about the following rock formations:

Giant's Causeway
Stone Mountain
Devil's Tower
Rock of Gibraltar
Garden of the Gods
Half Dome

Write a brief report about the formation that you find most interesting. In your report, you should tell where the rock formation is located, what type of rock it is composed of, how it was formed, and why it is interesting.

forces. However, under the steady force of wind, water, and temperature changes, the granite is slowly worn down. Bits of granite flake off. Dragged along in rushing streams, these bits of granite are reduced to sand.

The sand from the granite, along with other sediments, is carried by the streams to a river, which carries the sediments to the sea. As the river flows into the sea, its speed decreases and its load of sediments is deposited on the sea floor. Over the years, layers of sediment slowly pile up.

The weight of the upper layers puts pressure on the lower layers, pushing the particles closer together. Dissolved minerals—in this case, calcite—cement the particles together. What was once ground-up granite is now sandstone, a sedimentary rock.

As the layers of sandstone are buried under more and more layers of sediment, they are subjected to increasingly high temperatures and pressures. Under sufficiently high temperature and pressure, the particles in the sandstone are pressed even closer together until there are no spaces left between them. The calcite that cemented the grains together is replaced with silica (the main ingredient of the mineral quartz). The texture of the rock changes from grainy to smooth. It is now the metamorphic rock quartzite.

What happens next? One possibility is that the quartzite becomes molten deep inside the Earth. The resulting magma hardens back into granite. In time, the material in the newly formed granite may undergo the same steps of the rock cycle just described. But this is not the only possibility. What else might occur?

4–3 Section Review

1. What are the three main groups of rocks? Give one example from each group.
2. How are igneous rocks formed? Sedimentary rocks? Metamorphic rocks?
3. What is the rock cycle? What two factors in this cycle may change sandstone to quartzite?

Connection—*Architecture*
4. The sedimentary rocks limestone and sandstone are fairly good materials for building. But they do not wear as well as the metamorphic rocks—marble and quartzite—that are formed from them. Why do you think this is so? How might this affect an architect's choice of building materials?

FIND OUT BY DOING

Starting a Rock Collection

1. Label each specimen by putting a dot of light-colored paint in an inconspicuous place. When the paint dries, write a number on the dot of paint with permanent ink. (Start with the number 1 for the first specimen and work your way up.)

2. Prepare an index card for each specimen. This card should provide the following information about the specimen: its number, what it is, where it was found, and the date it was collected.

4–4 Fluid and Fire: Igneous Rocks

Guide for Reading

Focus on this question as you read.

▶ *How are igneous rocks classified?*

Igneous rocks are classified according to their composition and texture. Composition refers to the minerals of which rocks are formed. Texture means the shape, size, arrangement, and distribution of the minerals that make up rocks. Both composition and texture are evident in a rock's appearance. For example, light-colored igneous rocks are typically rich in the colorless mineral quartz, whereas dark-colored igneous rocks are typically rich in the dense, greenish gray mineral augite.

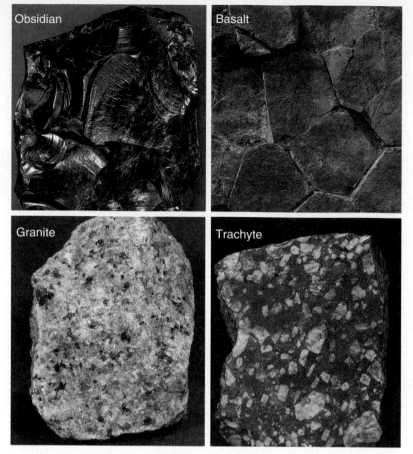

Figure 4–20 *Igneous rocks may be classified according to their texture. Trachyte has a porphyritic texture. What kind of textures are illustrated by obsidian, basalt, and granite?*

Obsidian

Basalt

Granite

Trachyte

FIND OUT BY

Mineral Deposits

This activity will help you to find out where some of the major mineral deposits in the world are located.

1. In the library, find a map of the world. Draw or trace the map on a sheet of paper. Label Africa, Asia, Europe, North America, South America, Australia, and Antarctica.

2. Find out where uranium, sulfur, aluminum, iron, halite, and gold deposits are located.

3. Using a symbol to represent each mineral, show the locations of these deposits on the map.

4. Make a key by writing the name of each mineral next to its symbol. Make your map colorful and descriptive.

As you can see in Figure 4–20 igneous rocks have four basic types of textures: glassy, fine-grained, coarse-grained, and porphyritic (por-fuh-RIHT-ihk). Glassy igneous rocks are shiny and look like glass. The materials that make up a glassy igneous rock are not organized into crystals. Obsidian (uhb-SIHD-ee-uhn), which is also known as volcanic glass, has a glassy texture.

Fine-grained rocks, unlike glassy rocks, are made of interlocking mineral crystals. These crystals are too small to be seen without the help of a microscope. The dark-gray rock known as basalt (buh-SAHLT) has a fine-grained texture.

Coarse-grained rocks, such as granite, consist of interlocking mineral crystals, which are all roughly the same size. The crystals in a coarse-grained rock are visible to the unaided eye.

Porphyritic rocks consist of large crystals scattered on a background of much smaller crystals. Sometimes these small background crystals are too tiny to be seen without a microscope. This gives some porphyritic rocks a texture that resembles rocky road ice cream.

Why do igneous rocks show such a variety of textures? Recall from Section 4–1 that how magma cools and where it cools determine the size of mineral crystals. The longer it takes magma to cool, the larger are the crystals that form. Glassy and fine-grained rocks form from lava that erupts from volcanoes and hardens on the Earth's surface. Coarse-grained rocks form from molten rock that cools and hardens within the Earth instead of at the Earth's surface.

Rocks formed from lava are called **extrusive** (ehk-STROO-sihv) **rocks.** Because lava is brought to the Earth's surface by volcanoes, extrusive rocks are also known as volcanic rocks. Basalt and obsidian are two kinds of extrusive rocks. Both these rocks are quite solid. In contrast, the gray volcanic glass called pumice (PUH-mihs) is filled with bubbles. Because pumice is filled with bubbles, it can float on water.

Igneous rocks formed deep within the Earth are called **intrusive** (ihn-TROO-sihv) **rocks.** They form when magma forces its way upward into preexisting rocks and then hardens. Intrusive rocks include granite and pegmatite, an extremely coarse-grained rock that may be rich in gemstones.

Intrusive rocks are also known as plutonic rocks, after Pluto, the Roman god of the underworld. A mass of intrusive rock is known as a pluton. As you can see in Figure 4–22 on page 100, plutons are classified according to their size, shape, and position relative to surrounding rocks.

Plutons may produce landforms by pushing up the layers of rock above them. This is how the domes you had read about in Chapter 1 are formed. Plutons may also produce landforms when the softer rock around them is worn away, exposing the buried intrusive rock.

Figure 4–21 *Molten rock may cool so quickly that gases inside do not have a chance to escape. The rock hardens around the bubbles, producing rocks that have more holes than Swiss cheese. Scoria is basically bubbly basalt (left). Pumice, a volcanic glass, is so light it can float on water (right).*

FIND OUT BY
DOING

An Igneous Invasion

Using papier-mâché, tempera paint, markers, a hardwood base, and any other materials necessary, make a model of an igneous rock intrusion. Use Figure 4–22 to help you make your model.

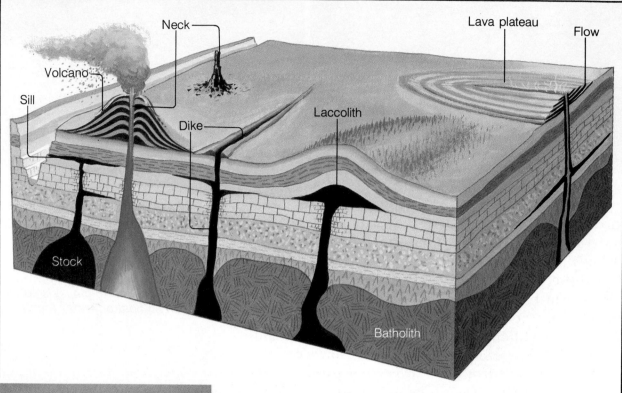

Figure 4–22 *Some igneous rock formations, such as volcanoes and lava plateaus, are visible on the surface as soon as they form. Most plutons, however, are revealed only after the surrounding rocks have worn away. The photograph shows two such formations in New Mexico. Shiprock is the exposed neck, or plug, of an ancient volcano. The Devil's Backbone is the remains of a dike.*

4–4 Section Review

1. What characteristics are used to classify igneous rocks?
2. How are intrusive rocks similar to extrusive rocks? How are they different?
3. What determines the size and type of crystals in rocks?
4. What is the relationship between a rock's texture and where it was formed?

Critical Thinking—*Developing a Hypothesis*
5. Propose an explanation for how porphyritic rocks are formed.

4–5 Slowly Built Layers: Sedimentary Rocks

Guide for Reading

Focus on this question as you read.

▶ *What are the different categories of sedimentary rocks?*

The most widely used classification system for sedimentary rocks places them into three main categories according to origin of the materials from which they are made. These three categories are: **clastic rocks, organic rocks,** and **chemical rocks.**

Clastic Rocks

Sedimentary rocks that are made of the fragments of previously existing rocks are known as clastic rocks. Clastic rocks are further classified according to the size and shape of the fragments in them.

Some clastic rocks are made of rounded pebbles cemented together by clay, mud, and sand. If over a third of the rock is made of pebbles, the rock is called a conglomerate (kahn-GLAHM-er-iht). The pebbles in conglomerates are smooth and rounded because they have been worn down by the action of water. Conglomerates are not as common as rocks made of smaller pieces because moving water tends to break large pieces into smaller pieces. Because they resemble an old-fashioned pudding filled with nuts and chopped fruit, conglomerates are sometimes called puddingstones.

Figure 4–23 *Clastic rocks are classified according to the size of the rock fragments they contain. Puddingstone and breccia have the largest fragments. How do the fragments in these two rocks differ? Sandstone is made up of sand-sized fragments. Shale is composed of dust-sized fragments.*

Clastic rocks made of small, sand-sized grains are called sandstones. At least half the particles in a clastic rock must be sand-sized in order for it to be considered a sandstone. Sandstones are very common rocks. They are formed from the sand on beaches, in riverbeds, and in sand dunes. In sandstones, the sand grains are cemented together by minerals. The minerals harden in the small spaces, or pores, between the grains.

Many geologists use the term shale to describe all the clastic rocks that are made of particles smaller than sand. Shales form from small particles of mud and clay that settle to the bottom of quiet bodies of water such as swamps. Most shales can be split into flat pieces.

Organic Rocks

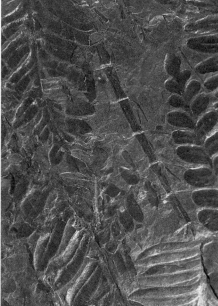

Organic rocks come from organisms; they are formed either directly or indirectly from material that was once living. Limestones, which are made of the mineral calcite, are often (but not always) organic rocks. Deposits of limestone may be formed from the limestone shells of creatures such as clams and certain microscopic one-celled organisms. When these organisms die, their shells collect on the ocean floor. Eventually, the shells are compacted into rock.

Living organisms may create limestone directly. Sometimes many animals with limestone shells live

Figure 4–24 *Coquina is composed primarily of fossil clam shells. The white cliffs of Dover are made of chalk. Coal is formed from the remains of plants that lived millions of years ago. When chunks of coal are broken apart, the ghostly impressions of ancient leaves may be revealed. To what group of sedimentary rocks do coquina, chalk, and coal belong?*

together. They cement their shells together and over time form large structures called reefs. Corals build limestone reefs off the coast of Florida and around many of the Caribbean and Pacific islands. Oysters build limestone reefs along the Texas Gulf coast.

Have you ever written or drawn with sticks of chalk? If so, you have first-hand experience with one kind of limestone. Chalk is a type of fine-grained limestone composed of microscopic shells, small fragments of shells, and calcite crystals. Because the particles in chalk are tiny and relatively loosely packed, chalk is much softer than other limestones.

Coal is another rock that is formed from the remains of living things. It is made from plants that lived millions of years ago.

Chemical Rocks

Some sedimentary rocks are formed when a sea or a lake dries up, leaving large amounts of minerals that were dissolved in the water. As you can see in Figure 4–25, the deposited minerals may create spectacular formations. Examples of chemical rocks formed in this way include rock salt and gypsum.

Some limestone rocks are formed by inorganic processes rather than by organisms. The strange and beautiful limestone formations found in many caves are formed by mineral-rich water dripping into the

FIND OUT BY
CALCULATING

Coral Conversions

The largest coral reef is the Great Barrier Reef, which parallels the northeastern coast of Australia for a distance of about 2000 kilometers. How many meters long is the Coral Reef? How many centimeters? Compare this distance to the distance across the United States, which is 4517 km from east to west.

Figure 4–25 *Chemical rocks form in many different places. As the sun beats down, evaporation forms strange towers of salt and calcium carbonate at Mono Lake, California. Spectacular formations are slowly built underground as water drips into a cave and deposits minerals.*

cave. When the water evaporates, a thin deposit of limestone is left behind. Over a long period of time, the deposits are built up into pillars, spikes, and other structures. Limestone may also be produced through chemical changes in ocean water that cause grains of calcite to form. The small grains get larger as additional thin layers are deposited from the ocean water. So these limestones are chemical rocks rather than organic rocks.

Figure 4–26 *Interesting sedimentary rock structures include geodes (top left), ripple marks (center left), concretions (bottom left), fossils (top right), and mud cracks (bottom right).*

4–5 Section Review

1. How are sedimentary rocks classified? Give an example of each major group.
2. What are clastic rocks? How are clastic rocks classified?
3. How are organic and chemical rocks similar? How are they different?

Critical Thinking—*Relating Concepts*
4. Explain how the fossil of a fish formed and ended up on the side of a mountain.

4–6 Changes in Form: Metamorphic Rocks

When already existing rocks are buried deep within the Earth, tremendous heat, great pressure, and chemical reactions may cause them to change into different rocks with different textures and structures. The changing of one type of rock into another as a result of heat, pressure, and/or chemical reactions is called **metamorphism** (meht-ah-MOR-fihz-uhm).

Figure 4–27 *Metamorphism may cause the minerals in a rock to separate into bands (right). It may also cause impurities in a rock to form minerals, such as garnets, that are not found in other types of rocks. Can you explain why schist (SHIHST), the most common metamorphic rock, may be dotted with garnets (left)?*

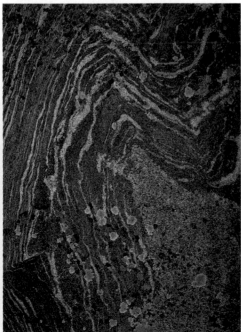

Shale

Slate

Granite

Gneiss

Metamorphic rocks may be formed from igneous, sedimentary, or metamorphic rocks. Although rocks remain solid during metamorphism, you can think of heat and pressure as making the rocks flexible enough to undergo change. Temperatures of about 100°C to 800°C cause some minerals to break down, allowing their atoms to form other, more heat-tolerant minerals. Under pressures hundreds or even thousands of times greater than at the Earth's surface, the atoms in rocks rearrange to form denser minerals. The combination of heat and pressure may cause the minerals in the rocks to separate into layers. Chemical reactions involving atoms from outside the original rocks may also occur. During metamorphism, a rock's texture, its mineral composition, and even its chemical composition may be changed.

The amount of heat, pressure, and chemical reactions varies during metamorphism. Thus the degree of metamorphism also varies. If the change in a rock is slight, some of the characteristics of the original rock can still be seen in the new rock. If the change in a rock is great, it may be difficult to tell what the original rock was. The characteristics of the original rock also affect the degree of metamorphism.

Figures 4–28 and 4–29 show some common metamorphic rocks. Each metamorphic rock is paired with one of the kinds of igneous or sedimentary rocks from which it is formed. Interestingly, many metamorphic rocks can be produced from more than one kind of rock. Slate, for example, can be formed from tuff, an igneous rock made of volcanic ash, as well as from shale.

Like igneous and sedimentary rocks, metamorphic rocks can be classified according to texture. The classification groups for metamorphic rocks are based on the arrangement of the grains that make up the rocks.

In the first group, the mineral crystals are arranged in parallel layers, or bands. These rocks are said to be foliated (FOH-lee-ay-tehd). The word foliated comes from the Latin word for leaf. It describes the layers in such metamorphic rocks, which

Figure 4–28 *Heat, pressure, and chemical reactions may transform one type of rock into another type of rock. How are metamorphic rocks classified?*

Figure 4–29 *Metamorphism may transform chalk (left) into marble (right). Marble is used to make tiles, rolling pins, and many other decorative and useful objects. Can you name some?*

are thin and flat, like leaves. Most metamorphic rocks are foliated. Foliated rocks—schist, slate, and gneiss, for example—tend to break along their bands.

In the second, smaller group of metamorphic rocks, the rocks are not banded and do not break into layers. These rocks are said to be unfoliated. Marble and quartzite are examples of unfoliated metamorphic rocks.

4–6 Section Review

1. Under what conditions do metamorphic rocks form?
2. What is metamorphism?
3. Name two metamorphic rocks. Name a rock from which each is formed.
4. How does pressure change rock?

Critical Thinking—*Relating Concepts*
5. Explain why metamorphism is often associated with intrusive igneous rocks and with tectonic plate collisions.

FIND OUT BY READING

Guides for the Perplexed

Confused by the enormous number of rocks and minerals? Don't despair—help is just a trip to the library or bookstore away! Many good field guides on rocks and minerals are available. Two of these are *Simon & Schuster's Guide to Rocks and Minerals* and *Simon & Schuster's Guide to Gems and Precious Stones.*

Laboratory Investigation

Creating Crystals

Problem

How do crystals form from liquids?

Materials *(per group)*

glass-marking pencil	dental floss
5 petri dishes	borax
250-mL beaker	alum
stirring rod	copper sulfate
table salt	magnifying glass

Procedure 🧪 📷

1. With the glass-marking pencil, label the petri dishes as shown in the accompanying diagram.

2. Using a beaker and stirring rod, dissolve 25 grams of table salt in 200 milliliters of hot water.

3. Fill a petri dish with this solution.

4. Place a piece of dental floss in the solution and let it hang over the edge of the dish.

5. Repeat steps 1 through 3 for borax, alum, and copper sulfate.

6. Allow the solutions to evaporate slowly for a day or two. Note which crystals form quickly and which form slowly.

7. With a magnifying glass, observe the crystals formed in the dish and along the dental floss.

Observations

1. Write a brief statement describing the results of this investigation.

2. Describe the appearance of each of the different crystals you grew.

Analysis and Conclusions

1. Prepare a graph that shows how long it took each of your crystals to grow.

2. Why do you think some crystals took longer than others to grow? How might you test your hypothesis?

3. Relate this investigation to sedimentary rock formation.

4. The minerals halite, kalinite, and hydrocyanite are composed from salt, alum, and copper sulfate, respectively. Are the crystals you made in this investigation minerals? Explain.

5. **On Your Own** Rock candy consists of clusters of large crystals of sugar. A wooden lollipop stick is often embedded in the rock candy. How do you think rock candy is made? Design an experiment to test your hypothesis. If you receive the proper permission, perform the experiment you have designed.

Study Guide

Summarizing Key Concepts

4–1 What Is a Mineral?

▲ A mineral is a naturally occurring, inorganic solid that has a definite chemical composition and crystal shape.

4–2 Uses of Minerals

▲ Ores are minerals from which metals and nonmetals can be removed in usable amounts.

4–3 What Is a Rock?

▲ A rock is a hard substance composed of one or more minerals.

▲ Igneous rocks are formed when hot, fluid rock cools and hardens.

▲ Most sedimentary rocks are formed from sediments that are compacted and/or cemented together.

▲ Metamorphic rocks are formed when chemical reactions, tremendous heat, and/or great pressure change existing rocks into new kinds of rocks.

▲ The continuous changing of rocks from one type to another is called the rock cycle.

4–4 Fluid and Fire: Igneous Rocks

▲ Igneous rocks are classified according to their composition and texture.

4–5 Slowly Built Layers: Sedimentary Rocks

▲ Many sedimentary rocks contain fossils.

▲ The most widely used classification system for sedimentary rocks places them into three main categories according to origin of the materials from which they are made. These three categories are: clastic rocks, organic rocks, and chemical rocks.

4–6 Changes in Form: Metamorphic Rocks

▲ Rocks that have been changed from an existing type of rock into a new type of rock are called metamorphic rocks.

Reviewing Key Terms

Define each term in a complete sentence.

4–1 What Is a Mineral?
mineral
inorganic
crystal
luster
hardness
streak
density
cleavage
fracture

4–2 Uses of Minerals
ore
metal

nonmetal
gemstone

4–3 What Is a Rock?
rock
igneous
sedimentary
sediment
metamorphic
rock cycle

4–4 Fluid and Fire: Igneous Rocks
extrusive rock
intrusive rock

4–5 Slowly Built Layers: Sedimentary Rocks
clastic rock
organic rock
chemical rock

4–6 Changes in Form: Metamorphic Rocks
metamorphism

Chapter Review

Content Review

Multiple Choice

Choose the letter of the answer that best completes each statement.

1. Metamorphic rocks with mineral crystals arranged in parallel layers, or bands, are
   a. clastic.
   b. intrusive.
   c. porphyritic.
   d. foliated.

2. The way in which a mineral reflects light from its surface is its
   a. streak.
   b. luster.
   c. fracture.
   d. brilliance.

3. Which rocks can be changed into sediments by weathering and erosion?
   a. sedimentary
   b. igneous
   c. metamorphic
   d. all of these

4. The two most common elements in the Earth's crust are
   a. oxygen and silicon.
   b. oxygen and nitrogen.
   c. sodium and iron.
   d. aluminum and magnesium.

5. The softest mineral in the Mohs hardness scale is
   a. fluorite.
   b. talc.
   c. diamond.
   d. calcite.

6. The breaking of a mineral along smooth, definite surfaces is called
   a. cleavage.
   b. fracture.
   c. splintering.
   d. foliation.

7. Which of these is an example of an intrusive rock?
   a. granite.
   b. basalt
   c. shale.
   d. obsidian

8. Elements that have shiny surfaces and are able to conduct electricity and heat are called
   a. metals.
   b. nonmetals.
   c. ores.
   d. gemstones.

True or False

If the statement is true, write "true." If it is false, change the underlined word or words to make the statement true.

1. A solid in which the atoms are arranged in a definite and repeating pattern is called a <u>crystal</u>.

2. Substances not formed from living things or the remains of living things are <u>organic</u>.

3. The color of the powder left by a mineral after it is rubbed against a hard, rough surface is called its <u>cleavage</u>.

4. The number <u>1</u> is assigned to the hardest mineral in the Mohs hardness scale.

5. Minerals from which metals and nonmetals can be removed in usable amounts are called <u>gemstones</u>.

Concept Mapping

Complete the following concept map for Section 4–1. Refer to pages J6–J7 to construct a concept map for the entire chapter.

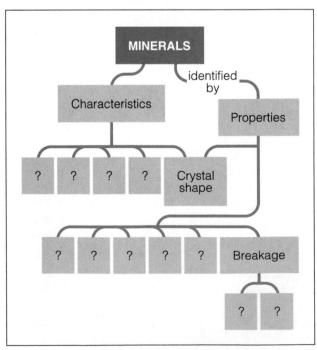

Concept Mastery

Discuss each of the following in a brief paragraph.

1. Describe eight properties used to identify minerals.
2. What are rock-forming minerals? Why are they important? List three examples of rock-forming minerals.
3. Relate the cooling rate of magma to the crystal size in igneous rocks.
4. Compare extrusive and intrusive igneous rocks. Give an example of each.
5. How can the shell of a snail become part of a sedimentary rock?
6. What is metamorphism? Describe how metamorphism affects three different kinds of rock.
7. What is a mineral? A rock?
8. What is the rock cycle? How are rocks changed into different forms in the rock cycle?

Critical Thinking and Problem Solving

Use the skills you have developed in this chapter to answer each of the following.

1. **Interpreting statements** Explain the following statement: You can determine the identity of a mineral by showing what it cannot be. Use specific properties of a mineral in your explanation.
2. **Relating concepts** Explain why scientists study sedimentary rocks to learn about prehistoric life.
3. **Developing a hypothesis** The gemstone opal is a sedimentary rock that consists of microscopic balls of silica (the main ingredient of quartz) cemented together by water and more silica. Explain how this opalized (changed to opal) fossil clam shell may have formed.

4. **Applying concepts** Obsidian and diorite are both igneous rocks. Obsidian looks like black glass. At a distance, diorite is dark gray; up close, it becomes clear that it is made of black, gray, and white grains. How do you account for the differences in these two rocks?
5. **Making inferences** Graphite and diamonds are both made of carbon. Yet they are not considered types of the same mineral. Rubies and sapphires are both made of aluminum oxide. They are considered types of the same mineral, corundum. Why do you think this is so?
6. **Identifying relationships** Suppose you have found a large mass of igneous rock between layers of sedimentary rock. Between the bottom of the igneous rock and the sedimentary rock you observe a thin layer of quartzite. The igneous rock itself is fine grained and very dark. What can you infer about the igneous formation's history?
7. **Using the writing process** Imagine that you are a particle of limestone. Write an autobiography entitled A Sedimental Journey, in which you describe your adventures as you travel through the rock cycle.

Weathering and Soil Formation

Guide for Reading

After you read the following sections, you will be able to

5–1 Weathering
- Distinguish between mechanical and chemical weathering.
- Recognize several factors that affect the rate of weathering.

5–2 Soil Formation
- Explain how soil is formed.

5–3 Soil Composition
- Identify the layers of mature soil.
- Recognize the importance of organic material and pore spaces to the quality of soil.

If you have ever been to the Black Hills of South Dakota, you have probably visited Mount Rushmore. Carved into a high granite cliff of this mountain are the faces of four famous presidents—George Washington, Thomas Jefferson, Abraham Lincoln, and Theodore Roosevelt. Since their completion in 1941, these carvings have attracted visitors from all over the world.

Yet several years ago, this beautiful monument was almost ruined. After a little more than forty years, the granite rock on these mammoth carvings was beginning to crumble. The presidents' faces were beginning to wear away. Trees and grass were sprouting from the head of George Washington! Worst of all, large pieces of the carved rock were falling off. Can you imagine what Lincoln would look like without his nose?

Luckily, workers for the National Park Service were able to save the monument before more serious damage occurred. Using plaster and metal spikes, they were able to keep the presidents' faces from crumbling. But what had made hard, solid granite crumble and crack? As you read this chapter, you will discover the answer.

Journal *Activity*

You and Your World Plant a few seeds in a pot of soil. It does not make much difference what seeds you plant. Keep the soil moist, but not too wet. Watch the pot for several weeks. Record your observations, either as words or as drawings, in your journal.

◄ *This National Park Service worker is repairing damage to the Mount Rushmore National Memorial caused by weathering. Look below the worker to see where a crack in President Lincoln's nose has been filled with plaster.*

5–1 Weathering

The reason the rocks of Mount Rushmore—as well as many other natural features of the Earth's surface—have cracked and crumbled is that the Earth's surface is constantly undergoing a natural breaking-down process. **The breaking down of rocks and other materials on the Earth's surface is called weathering.** A slow, continuous process, **weathering** affects all substances exposed to the atmosphere.

Because weathering of rocks is such a slow process, the effects are not always easily observed. But other types of weathering are more obvious. You have probably seen the effects of weathering if you have ever noticed paint peeling on the side of a house. Or perhaps you have noticed changes that occur on a brick building. New bricks have a bright red color and sharp corners and edges. The bricks of an old building are darker in color. The corners and edges are rounded. Pieces of the bricks may have broken off.

As you have just read, rocks on the Earth's surface also undergo weathering. Large pieces often break off the rocks. Over a long period of time, the rocks crumble and decay. You can see the results of weathering at the base of a mountain or on a mountain slope. Pieces of broken rocks pile up in these areas. These piles of rock fragments are called talus (TAY-luhs) slopes.

Rocks on the Earth's surface are broken down by two types of weathering. When the forces of

Figure 5–1 *The effects of weathering often take only a short time to become evident—as you may know if you have ever left a bicycle or roller skates out in the rain! Rust, which results from weathering, may appear quite quickly on exposed metal objects (right). Most of the time, however, weathering takes a long time. It took thousands of years for this talus slope in Glacier National Park in Montana to form (left). How does a talus slope form?*

weathering break rocks into smaller pieces but do not change the chemical makeup of the rocks, the process is called mechanical weathering. When the chemical makeup of the rocks is changed, the process is called chemical weathering.

Mechanical Weathering

During **mechanical weathering,** rocks are broken into different shapes and smaller pieces. At the beginning of the weathering process, typical rock fragments are sharp and angular. As weathering continues, they become smooth and rounded. Although there are several different agents, or causes, of mechanical weathering, each results in the breaking down of rocks.

TEMPERATURE Rocks can be broken apart by changes in temperature. During the day, rocks on the Earth's surface are heated by the sun's rays. The outside of the rock heats up and begins to expand. But the inside of the rock remains cool and does not expand. When the air temperature drops at night, the outside of the rock cools and contracts.

The next day, the heat from the sun causes the outside of the rock to expand again. The cycle of heating and cooling continues. The repeated changes in temperature cause particles on the surface of the rock to crack or flake off. Often the pieces break off in curved sheets or slabs parallel to the rock's surface. This type of breaking off of rock is called **exfoliation** (ehks-foh-lee-AY-shuhn). Other agents of mechanical weathering also cause exfoliation.

FROST ACTION Unlike most liquids, water expands when it freezes. The repeated freezing and melting of water is a common cause of mechanical weathering. This process of weathering is called **frost action.**

Frost action occurs when water seeps into a small opening or crack in a rock. When the temperature falls below 0°C, the freezing point of water, the water in the crack freezes and expands. The crack in the rock is made larger by the pressure of the expanding water. In time, the freezing and melting of the water cause the rock to break into pieces. The cracks and potholes you see in roads or in cement driveways are often the result of frost action.

Figure 5–2 *Pieces of this granite rock in Yosemite National Park in California are flaking off in curved sheets parallel to the rock's surface. What is this process called? What causes it?*

FIND OUT BY DOING

Expanding Water

1. Fill a clear plastic container about three-fourths full of water. Mark the water level on the outside of the container. Use a piece of tape or a marking pencil.

2. Place the water-filled container in the freezer for at least 6 hours.

3. Remove the container and observe the level of the ice that has formed. Explain your observations.

■ Develop a plan to use frozen water to break up large rocks.

Figure 5–3 *As this cedar tree grows, its roots pry apart the boulder on which it is growing. What is this type of mechanical weathering called?*

ORGANIC ACTIVITY Plants and animals can cause mechanical weathering. The roots of plants sometimes loosen rock material. A plant growing in a crack in a rock can make the crack larger as the plant's roots grow and spread out. This type of mechanical weathering is called **root-pry.** Root-pry is an organic activity, or an activity caused by living things.

GRAVITY Gravity is another agent of mechanical weathering. Sometimes gravity pulls loosened rocks down mountain cliffs in a **landslide.** A landslide is a large movement of loose rocks and soil. As the rocks fall, they collide with one another and break into smaller pieces. Falling rocks generally occur in areas where a road or highway has been cut through a rock formation, leaving cliffs on one or both sides of the road.

ABRASION Wind-blown sand causes mechanical weathering of rocks by **abrasion** (uh-BRAY-zhuhn). Abrasion is the wearing away of rocks by solid particles carried by wind, water, or other forces. In desert regions, the wind easily picks up and moves sand particles. The sharp edges of the sand particles scrape off small pieces of exposed rocks. Over a long period of time, the abrading sand can create unusual shapes in exposed rocks. See Figure 5–4.

Water also causes abrasion of rocks. Running water such as a river carries along loose rocks and other particles. The moving rocks and particles collide,

Figure 5–4 *Mechanical weathering can tear down the sides of mountains or wear away rocks to produce unusual formations. What agent of mechanical weathering caused this road-blocking landslide to occur (right)? How were the "Sunbonnet Rock" and "Navaho Twins" formed (left)?*

scrape against one another, and eventually break. In addition, the moving rocks scrape the rocks in the riverbed. This action makes riverbed rocks smooth and rounded.

Chemical Weathering

During **chemical weathering,** changes occur in the mineral composition, or chemical makeup, of rocks. As chemical changes take place, minerals can be added to or removed from rocks. Or the minerals in rocks can be broken down in a process called decomposition. Many substances react chemically with rocks to break them down.

WATER Most chemical weathering is caused by water and carbon dioxide. (You will learn more about the action of carbon dioxide on the next page.) Water can dissolve most of the minerals that hold rocks together. Rocks that dissolve in water are said to be soluble.

Water can also form acids when it mixes with certain gases in the atmosphere. These acids often speed up the decomposition of rocks. Water can also combine with a mineral to form a completely different mineral. For example, when the mineral feldspar reacts with water, it forms clay.

OXIDATION Chemical weathering is also caused by **oxidation** (ahk-suh-DAY-shuhn). Oxidation is the process in which oxygen chemically combines with another substance. The result of oxidation is the formation of an entirely different substance.

Figure 5–5 *Oxidation has turned the rocks red in the Valley of Fire, Nevada. Water may dissolve away solid limestone to form vast networks of underground caverns. Can you explain how chemical weathering at the surface resulted in the formation of stalactites and stalagmites within this cave?*

Weathering in Action

1. Place a piece of steel wool outside your school in an area where it will be exposed to the air.

2. Place another piece of steel wool in a sheltered place in your classroom.

3. Examine both pieces of steel wool daily for one month. Record your observations each day.

What changes do you observe? What are the conditions that contributed to these differences?

■ Devise a way to protect a piece of steel wool from weathering. With your teacher's help, plan an investigation to see if your method of protection works.

Figure 5–6 *Lichens, like plants, are living things that can release weak acids into their environment. How do these lichens affect the rock on which they grow?*

Iron in rocks combines with oxygen in the air to form iron oxide, or rust. This is one example of chemical weathering by oxidation. The color of some rocks is an indication that oxidation is occurring. If oxidation is taking place, the inner material of a rock will be a different color from the outer material. What color is iron rust?

CARBONATION When carbon dioxide dissolves in water, a weak acid called carbonic acid is formed. Carbonic acid is the acid used to give soft drinks their fizz. When carbonic acid reacts chemically with other substances, the process of **carbonation** occurs.

In nature carbonic acid is formed when carbon dioxide in the air dissolves in rain. This slightly acidic rain falls to the ground and sinks into the soil. The carbonic acid is able to dissolve certain rocks on or beneath the surface of the Earth. Fortunately, carbonic acid is too weak to be harmful to plants and animals. But it does slowly wear away feldspars and limestone.

SULFURIC ACID The air in certain areas is polluted with sulfur oxides. Sulfur oxides are a byproduct of the burning of coal as a source of energy. These compounds dissolve in rainwater to form sulfuric acid. Rain that contains sulfuric acid is one type of acid rain. Sulfuric acid is a much stronger acid than carbonic acid. Sulfuric acid corrodes, or wears away, rocks, metals, and other materials very quickly. What effects do you predict sulfuric acid would have on monuments and buildings?

PLANT ACIDS You have read before that plants can be agents of mechanical weathering. Plants can also cause chemical weathering. Plants produce weak acids that dissolve certain minerals in rocks.

For example, mosses produce weak acids. Mosses are low-growing plants that resemble a soft green carpet. Mosses often grow in damp areas. As they grow, the acids they produce seep into rocks and dissolve some of the minerals. At some point, the rocks break into smaller pieces. Lichens are another type of living thing that produces weak acids capable of dissolving the minerals in rocks. The chemical weathering produced by mosses and lichens is important in the formation of soil.

Rate of Weathering

The rate of weathering, or how fast weathering takes place, depends on several factors. One factor is the composition of the rocks. Two different types of rock in the same climate can weather differently, depending on the minerals that make up each rock type. If the minerals in a rock resist chemical weathering, the rock is called a **stable rock.**

The stability of a rock can vary, depending on the climate in which that rock is found. Limestone, for example, weathers very little in a dry, warm climate. But in a wet climate, moisture can completely dissolve limestone.

Granite is a very stable rock in cool, dry climates. But in tropical climates, granite crumbles easily. The abundant rainfall dissolves much of the mineral feldspar, which holds granite together. The feldspar becomes loose clay, which is too weak to keep the rock from breaking apart. The more moisture there is in an area, the more quickly rocks will weather.

The amount of time that rock is exposed on the Earth's surface also affects its rate of weathering. A very old rock that has not been exposed to the various forces of weathering can remain almost unchanged. But if a newly formed rock is immediately deposited on the Earth's surface, it will begin to weather right away.

The amount of exposed surface area on a rock also affects its rate of weathering. As rocks are broken down into many small pieces, more rock surfaces are exposed and more weathering takes place. In rocks that contain many joints or cracks, various chemicals easily come in contact with the rock surfaces and break them down.

Weathering Rates

1. Place an antacid tablet inside a folded piece of paper. Put on safety goggles. Carefully tap the tablet with a hammer until the tablet has broken into small pieces.

2. Place the broken tablet in a glass. Place an unbroken tablet in another glass.

3. Add 10 mL of water to both glasses at the same time. Observe both reactions until they are finished. Record your observations.

What differences in the rate of reaction did you observe?

■ What relationship can you identify from the activity?

■ Develop a hypothesis that relates the results of this activity to the weathering process in nature.

Figure 5–7 *Granite weathers slowly in the cool, dry climate of Yosemite National Park (left). In tropical climates, granite weathers more quickly (right).*

1. What is weathering? Describe the two types.
2. In what two ways do plants contribute to the weathering of rocks?
3. Identify several factors that influence the rate at which weathering occurs.

Connection—*Ecology*
4. A limestone statue of a dog is placed in a park in Miami, Florida. What types of natural forces would affect the weathering of this statue?

Guide for Reading

Focus on this question as you read.

▶ How does soil form?

Figure 5–8 *Almost all living things depend on soil. Plants require minerals from the soil in order to live and grow. Why is this bison, as well as other animals, dependent on soil? Many living things make their home in the soil. The mole's broad, shovel-shaped paws are just one adaptation for its life underground.*

5–2 Soil Formation

The weathering of rocks on the Earth's surface results in the formation of soil. **Soil is formed when rocks are continuously broken down by weathering.** As rocks weather, they break into smaller pieces. These pieces are broken down into even smaller pieces to form soil.

The formation of soil is extremely important to most living organisms. Plants depend on soil directly as a source of food. Soil supplies plants with minerals and water needed for growth. Animals depend on soil indirectly for the materials they need to live. Some animals eat plants; other animals eat animals that eat plants. You may already know that a lion

eats other animals. But even a mighty lion depends on plants that grow in soil. The zebras and gnus that are food for a lion eat plants. In this way a lion depends on soil for its survival.

Sometimes soil remains on top of its parent rock, or the rock from which it was formed. This soil is called **residual** (rih-ZIHJ-oo-uhl) **soil.** Residual soil has a composition similar to that of the parent rock it covers. Some soil is moved away from its parent rock by water, wind, glaciers, and waves. Soil that is moved away from its place of origin is called **transported soil.** Transported soil can be very different in composition from the layer of rock it covers. In either case, the layer of rock beneath the soil is called **bedrock.**

Living organisms help to form soil. Some organisms produce acids that chemically break down rocks. Mosses and lichens are two examples that you should recall from the previous section. Certain bacteria in the soil cause the decay of dead plants and animals. Decay is the breaking down of plants and animals into the substances they are made of. This decaying material is called **humus** (HYOO-muhs). Humus is a dark-colored material that is important for the growth of plants. Some of the chemicals

FIND OUT BY DOING

Humus

1. Obtain some topsoil from a forest or a grassy area. You may even be able to get a sample of topsoil from a garden center.

2. Carefully sort through the soil. Use a magnifying glass to separate the small particles of soil from the particles of organic material.

What types of soil particles are in your sample? What kinds of organic particles are in your topsoil?

Figure 5–9 *Soil formation begins when solid parent rock is broken down into smaller pieces by weathering (left). As weathering continues, the rock is broken down further into soil particles (center). Under certain conditions, a thick layer of soil will develop above the parent rock (right).*

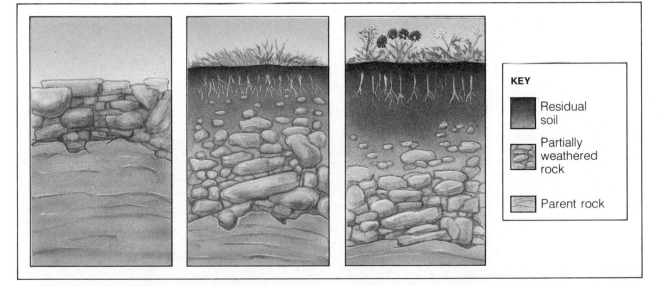

KEY

Residual soil

Partially weathered rock

Parent rock

PROBLEM Solving

Plants in Pots

José and Carol spent a day in a commercial greenhouse. Walking up and down the rows of plants, the two friends noticed that different kinds of soils were used to grow various plants. For example, the soil in pots that had cactuses growing was very sandy. The pots that held tropical plants had a dark brown soil rich in humus.

On their return home, the two friends wondered about their observations. What could explain the differences they observed in the kinds of soils used to grow different plants?

Designing an Experiment

Design an investigation to determine if the kind of soil used to grow a particular kind of plant is important. If you decide to do this investigation and have your teacher's approval, keep a picture record of your observations.

produced during the process of decay speed up the breakdown of rocks into soil.

Living things such as moles, earthworms, ants, and beetles help to break apart large pieces of soil as they burrow through the ground. The burrows allow water to move rapidly through the soil. The water speeds up weathering of the underlying rock.

5–2 Section Review

1. How is soil formed?
2. Compare residual soil and transported soil.
3. What is humus? Why is it important for plant growth?

Critical Thinking—*Applying Concepts*

4. Plants get water and minerals needed for growth from soil. What do animals get from soil?

5–3 Soil Composition

Pieces of weathered rock and organic material, or humus, are the two main ingredients of soil. Organic material is material that was once living or was formed by the activity of living organisms. Rock particles form more than 80 percent of soil. Air and water are also present in soil.

Clay and quartz are the most abundant minerals in soil. Because clay and quartz are very stable minerals, they exist in the greatest quantities. Potassium, phosphorus, and the nitrogen compounds called nitrates are other important minerals in soil. Because these three minerals are vital to plant growth, they are included in the fertilizers added to soil.

Air and water fill the spaces between soil particles. These spaces are called **pore spaces.** Plants and animals use the water and air in these spaces, as well as the minerals dissolved in the water. Pore spaces are important for healthy plant roots. Plant roots need oxygen, which they get from the air in the pore spaces.

The composition of soil varies from place to place. The type of rock broken down by weathering determines the kinds of minerals in the soil. For example, soil formed largely from a parent rock of limestone will be different from soil formed from a parent rock of sandstone.

The type of weathering also affects the composition of soil. Mechanical weathering produces soil with a composition similar to the rock being weathered. Chemical weathering produces soil with a composition different from that of the rock being weathered. Why do you think this is so?

Soil Texture

The type of weathering also affects soil texture. Texture refers to the size of individual soil particles. Soil particles vary from very small to large.

Both mechanical and chemical weathering first break rocks down into gravel. Gravel particles are between 2 and 64 millimeters in diameter. Both types of weathering then break gravel down into

Guide for Reading

Focus on these questions as you read.
▶ *What are the two main ingredients of soil?*
▶ *What are some characteristics of each soil horizon?*

Figure 5–10 *The reddish, sandy soil is low in humus. How can you tell that the silty clay soil is high in humus?*

sand. Sand particles are less than 2 millimeters in diameter.

Silt is made of very small broken crystals of rock formed in the same way as sand is. Silt particles are less than 1/16 of a millimeter in diameter. Clay is the smallest soil particle produced by chemical and mechanical weathering. Clay particles are smaller than silt particles. They are, in fact, less than 1/256 millimeter in diameter.

Soil Horizons

As soil forms, it develops separate soil layers called horizons (huh-RIGH-zuhns). Each soil **horizon** is different. Imagine making a vertical slice through these horizons. You would observe one horizon piled on top of another. Such a view is called a cross section. A cross section of the soil horizons is called a **soil profile.** A soil profile shows the different layers of soil. A soil profile is shown in Figure 5–11.

Soil that has developed three layers is called mature soil. It takes many thousands of years and the proper conditions for soil to develop three layers. Some soil contains only two layers. This soil is called immature soil. Immature soil has been formed more recently than mature soil has.

Figure 5–11 *As soil forms, it develops distinct layers called horizons (right). What horizons can you identify in the forest soil profile (left)?*

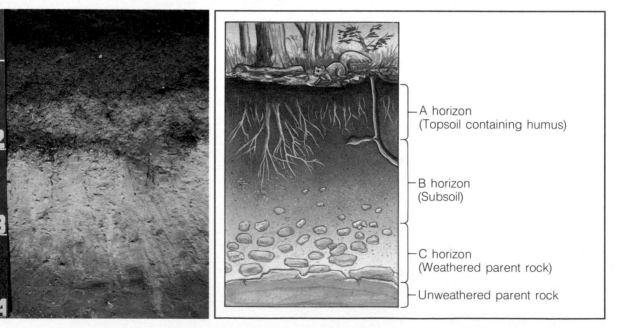

The uppermost layer of mature soil is called the A horizon. The A horizon is a dark-colored soil layer in which much activity by living organisms takes place. Bacteria, earthworms, beetles, and other organisms in this horizon constantly add to the soil through the process of decay. These organisms also break apart large pieces of soil as they move through the ground.

The soil in the A horizon is called **topsoil**. Topsoil consists mostly of humus and other organic materials. Humus supplies minerals essential for plant growth. Because humus is spongy, it stores water. It also contains many pore spaces through which air and water can reach plant roots. Topsoil is the most fertile part of the soil. Plants are able to grow well in the fertile, or nutrient-rich, soil of the A horizon.

Water that soaks into the ground washes some minerals from the A horizon into the second layer of soil, or the B horizon. This process is called **leaching** (LEECH-ihng). The B horizon is just below the A horizon. In addition to leached-out minerals, the B horizon is made of clay and some humus. The soil in the B horizon is called **subsoil**. Subsoil is formed very slowly. The B horizon may take more than 100,000 years to form!

The third layer of soil is called the C horizon. The C horizon consists of partly weathered rock. The C horizon extends down to the top of the un-weathered parent rock. The composition of soil in the C horizon is similar to that of the parent rock.

Whether all three soil horizons develop depends on several factors. Time is one of the most important factors in soil formation. The longer a rock is exposed to the forces of weathering, the more it is broken down. Mature soil is formed if all three layers have had time to develop.

In some places, the upper layers of soil are removed, and the rocks below the soil are exposed. The weathering process then forms new soil from the exposed rocks. This recently formed soil is immature because there has not been enough time for all three soil layers to form. For example, soil in the northern regions, where glacial erosion has taken place, is immature soil. The glaciers that covered the area removed much of the soil from the top horizons. Since then, weathering has produced new soil.

Figure 5–12 *A backyard garden can be a source of vegetables, flowers, and fun. How does the soil in a garden affect the plants grown there? Why do many people add topsoil to their garden?*

FIND OUT BY DOING

Studying a Soil Profile

1. Use a shovel to dig down about 0.5 m to obtain a soil sample from your yard or from a yard in your neighborhood. Remember to ask permission before you begin to dig. Try not to disturb the soil too much, or you will not be able to observe the different soil layers.

2. Observe the soil sample. Answer the following questions:

a. How deep is the topsoil layer? What color is it?

b. How deep is the subsoil layer? What color is it?

c. How does the soil in the two layers differ?

d. Did you find the layer of parent rock? If so, describe this layer.

■ Is your soil sample mature soil?

Figure 5–13 *The soil that once covered this rock has been removed by large moving sheets of ice known as glaciers. The broad horizontal groove in the rock was carved by a large stone embedded in the bottom of a slowly moving glacier (right). Soil may also be removed by the action of heavy rains or floods (left).*

Climate is another important factor in the formation of soil. In areas with heavy rainfall and warm temperatures, weathering takes place more rapidly. Organisms are more plentiful in the soil in these areas. They speed up the chemical and mechanical weathering of rocks. Heavy rainfall in tropical regions of the world washes much of the topsoil away. But because many plants and animals live in this climate, soil that is washed away is replaced quickly.

The type of rock in an area also affects soil formation. Some rocks do not weather as rapidly as others do. Rocks that do not break down easily do not form soil rapidly. For example, in some climates it takes a long time for granite to break down. So soil formation from granite in these climates is relatively slow. But sandstone breaks and crumbles into sand very quickly. Soil formation from the weathering of sandstone is rapid.

The surface features of the region also determine the speed at which soil is formed. On very steep slopes, rainwater drains rapidly. The rainwater does not have a chance to sink into the soil layers, so little weathering takes place.

Blowing Sands

One of the great tragedies of the first half of the twentieth century was the creation of the dust bowl. John Steinbeck wrote about the lives of people who lived in the area of the dust bowl in a powerful novel called *The Grapes of Wrath*. You might like to read this moving novel that details the triumph of the human spirit over disastrous living conditions.

5–3 Section Review

1. What is a soil horizon?
2. Describe a typical soil profile.
3. What two factors affect soil composition?

Critical Thinking—*Relating Concepts*
4. Some people buy topsoil from a garden center to add to their own garden soil. Why is this added topsoil beneficial for plant growth?

CONNECTIONS

A Search for Soil to Produce Food

If you could fly over a *tropical rain forest,* you would notice a thick covering of trees. In fact, the trees grow so thick that you would not see the plants that grow low to the ground. And obviously, from the air, you wouldn't even catch the tiniest glimpse of the soil.

From your observations, you might logically conclude that the soil in a tropical rain forest is rich and fertile—good soil for plants to grow in. If you were a farmer, it might seem to you that the land here could produce abundant crops.

Appearances in a tropical rain forest are deceiving, however. When the forest is cleared to make room for crops or for pastures, something strange and terrible happens.

The first year or two, crops or grasses grow well. But with each successive year, the growth of the crops or grasses is greatly diminished. The soil loses its fertility, and the loss is permanent. Why does this happen?

The answer lies in two apparent opposites: fire and rain. Tropical forests are cleared by what is called a *slash-and-burn* technique. The ashes from the burned forest act like fertilizer, adding minerals to the soil. This is why crops and grasses can be grown on newly cleared areas. In a year or two, however, heavy rains wash the minerals from the soil. The rains even wash away the soil itself. In between the rains, the soil bakes in the sun and develops a hard crust that discourages plant growth.

The rains are not a problem in an undisturbed tropical rain forest. There, the loss of minerals is balanced by the formation of humus. The thick vegetation prevents soil from washing away. The native plants also keep the soil moist and loose, so a crust does not form.

But rains eventually destroy the land that was cleared for cropland and pastures. More forest lands are slashed-and-burned, and this sad cycle continues. Meanwhile, the abandoned fields and pastures become scrubland or deserts.

Laboratory Investigation

Observing the Effect of Chemical Weathering on Rocks

Problem

What rocks are affected by carbonated water—a form of carbonic acid?

Materials *(per group)*

8 baby food jars
carbonated water
masking tape
2 fragments of each of the following rocks:
   limestone, marble, granite, sandstone

Procedure

1. Fill four baby food jars three-fourths full of carbonated water. Fill the remaining four baby food jars three-fourths full of tap water. Carefully place the jars on your desk.

2. Use masking tape to label the jars: limestone and carbonated water, limestone and tap water, marble and carbonated water, marble and tap water, granite and carbonated water, granite and tap water, sandstone and carbonated water, sandstone and tap water.

3. Place the appropriate rock fragment into each labeled jar.

4. Observe the effects. Record your observations in a chart similar to the one shown.

5. Continue to observe the rock specimens. After 20 minutes, record your observations again.

6. Let the jars stand overnight. Observe them again the next day. Record any changes in the rock fragments.

Observations

1. Which samples show that a change has taken place?

2. For each sample, how did the effects produced by carbonated water compare with the effects produced by tap water?

Analysis and Conclusions

1. What evidence supports the idea that a chemical change has occurred?

2. What is the effect of time on the rate of weathering?

3. How does carbonic acid affect rocks?

4. **On Your Own** Obtain some other rock samples. Perform a similar investigation to determine the effect of carbonic acid on these rock samples. Then using all your rock samples, design an experiment to determine whether temperature has an effect on chemical weathering.

Rock	Carbonated Water			Tap Water		
	Initial	20 min	24 hr	Initial	20 min	24 hr
Limestone						
Marble						
Granite						
Sandstone						

Study Guide

Summarizing Key Concepts

5–1 Weathering

▲ Mechanical weathering causes rocks to be broken into smaller pieces, but the chemical makeup of the rocks is not changed.

▲ The agents of mechanical weathering are temperature, frost action, organic activity, gravity, and abrasion.

▲ Chemical weathering causes a change in the mineral composition of rocks.

▲ Chemical weathering is caused by water, oxidation, carbonation, sulfuric acid, and acids produced by plants.

▲ The rate of weathering depends on the composition of the rock, the amount of time the rock is exposed on the Earth's surface, and the amount of exposed surface area of the rock.

5–2 Soil Formation

▲ Soil is formed when rocks are continuously broken down by weathering.

▲ Soil forms above a solid layer of rock called bedrock.

▲ Residual soil remains on top of its parent rock. Transported soil is moved from its place of origin.

▲ Humus is the material formed from the decay of plants and animals.

5–3 Soil Composition

▲ The two main ingredients of soil are pieces of weathered rock and organic material.

▲ Air and water fill the pore spaces between particles of soil.

▲ The type of rocks broken down by weathering determines the kinds of minerals in the soil.

▲ As soil forms, it develops separate layers, or horizons. A cross section of the soil horizons is called a soil profile.

▲ A typical soil profile has an A horizon, or topsoil, a B horizon, or subsoil, and a C horizon.

Reviewing Key Terms

Define each term in a complete sentence.

5–1 Weathering
weathering
mechanical weathering
exfoliation
frost action
root-pry
landslide
abrasion
chemical weathering
oxidation
carbonation
stable rock

5–2 Soil Formation
residual soil
transported soil
bedrock
humus

5–3 Soil Composition
pore space
horizon
soil profile
topsoil
leaching
subsoil

Chapter Review

Content Review

Multiple Choice

Choose the letter of the answer that best completes each statement.

1. The breaking off of rock pieces in curved sheets parallel to the rock's surface is
   a. oxidation.
   c. root-pry.
   b. carbonation.
   d. exfoliation.
2. Rocks can be broken apart by
   a. organic activity.
   c. frost action.
   b. root-pry.
   d. all of these.
3. The wearing away of rocks by solid particles carried by wind, water, and other forces is called
   a. exfoliation.
   c. oxidation.
   b. abrasion.
   d. gravity.
4. Most chemical weathering is caused by
   a. air pollution.
   c. sulfuric acid.
   b. water.
   d. gravity.
5. The decayed parts of plants and animals in soil are called
   a. humus.
   c. residual soil.
   b. topsoil.
   d. mature soil.
6. If the minerals in a rock enable the rock to resist chemical weathering, the rock is described as
   a. stable.
   c. organic.
   b. soluble.
   d. residual.
7. The solid rock layer beneath the soil is called
   a. transported soil.
   c. residual rock.
   b. bedrock.
   d. mature soil.
8. The size of individual soil particles is called soil
   a. profile.
   c. texture.
   b. horizon.
   d. porosity.
9. The process in which water washes minerals from one soil horizon to another is called
   a. leaching.
   c. exfoliation.
   b. oxidation.
   d. claying.

True or False

If the statement is true, write "true." If it is false, change the underlined word or words to make the statement true.

1. When gravity pulls loosened rocks down a mountain cliff, a <u>landslide</u> occurs.
2. When the chemical makeup of rocks is changed, <u>mechanical</u> weathering occurs.
3. A rock that <u>dissolves</u> easily in water is said to be <u>stable</u>.
4. Rain that contains <u>humus</u> is called acid rain.
5. <u>Transported</u> soil has a composition similar to that of the bedrock it covers.
6. <u>Clay and quartz</u> are the most abundant minerals in soil.
7. The largest particles found in soil are <u>silt</u>.
8. The soil in the B horizon is called <u>topsoil</u>.

Concept Mapping

Complete the following concept map for Section 5–1. Refer to pages J6–J7 to construct a concept map for the entire chapter.

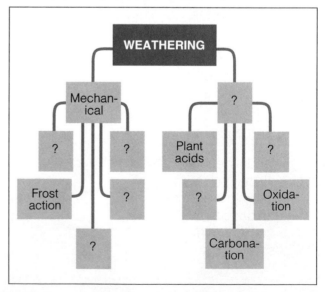

Concept Mastery

Discuss each of the following in a brief paragraph.

1. What is the difference between mechanical and chemical weathering?
2. How is the weathering of rocks helpful to life on Earth?
3. Briefly describe how soil is formed.
4. What is acid rain? How does it contribute to weathering?
5. Some scientists say the "soil is alive." What does this statement mean?
6. What is the difference between residual soil and transported soil?
7. Why are pore spaces important for good plant growth?
8. How does weathering affect the texture of soil?
9. Describe a typical soil profile.
10. Compare the following types of soil particles: gravel, sand, silt, and clay.

Critical Thinking and Problem Solving

Use the skills you have developed in this chapter to answer each of the foillowing.

1. **Relating concepts** Why would frost action not be a major cause of weathering in polar climates?
2. **Making predictions** Predict what would happen if you rubbed a piece of granite with sandpaper. If you rubbed a piece of sandstone. What type of weathering is simulated in this activity?
3. **Analyzing data** In an experiment to measure soil's ability to hold water, particle size and the amount of humus the soil contained were tested. The accompanying data table shows the results.

   Use the data to construct a graph that represents the relationship between the amount of water retained and the size of the soil particles.

   Based on your graph, describe a type of soil that would supply water for plant roots during a period of little rainfall.

4. **Making inferences** How would you determine if a soil was formed by mechanical or by chemical weathering?
5. **Relating concepts** If you overwater a potted plant for a period of time, the plant will probably die. However, in nature plants do not usually die after periods of heavy rain. Explain why this is so.
6. **Using the writing process** Many farmers and scientists are concerned that topsoil is being washed away from the land at a dangerous rate. They feel that we are in danger of losing one of our most valuable assets. Yet few people outside the scientific and farming community seem concerned. Write a letter to your representative in Congress, voicing your concern about this problem. Make sure you explain why it is important to protect our valuable soil resources.

	Small Particles		Medium Particles		Large Particles	
	With humus	**Without humus**	**With humus**	**Without humus**	**With humus**	**Without humus**
Water retained by soil	50.0 mL	20.8 mL	44.6 mL	13.6 mL	39.8 mL	10.2 mL

Erosion and Deposition

6

Guide for Reading

After you read the following sections, you will be able to

6–1 Changing the Earth's Surface
- ■ Define the terms erosion and deposition.

6–2 Gravity
- ■ Describe the types of erosion caused by gravity.

6–3 Wind
- ■ Identify the effects of wind erosion and deposition.

6–4 Running Water
- ■ Explain why water is the major cause of erosion.

6–5 Glaciers
- ■ Distinguish among the different features of glacial deposition.

6–6 Waves
- ■ Describe the changes in the Earth's surface caused by waves.

To the people of the Huaylas Valley, the glacier (a huge mass of ice and snow perched on the steep northwest face of Peru's highest peak) was a familiar sight. The people hardly took notice of the glacier. It had been there for as long as they could remember—creeping forward when fed by winter snows and shrinking back when warmed by summer temperatures. For this glacier, named Glacier 511 by Peruvian geologists, was only one of hundreds that dotted the Andes Mountains.

Then at 6:13 PM on January 10, 1962, Glacier 511 stirred. A great mass of ice about 182 meters long and nearly 1 kilometer wide broke loose. As it hurtled down the cliff, it picked up tons of rock material. It plowed up chunks of granite as large as houses. It swept up everything in its path. Within 8 minutes, the wall of ice, snow, rock, and mud had covered a distance of 16 kilometers and buried an estimated 4000 people from 9 villages. It had demonstrated the awesome power of moving ice.

Glaciers—along with winds, waves, running water, and gravity—constantly reshape the Earth's surface. In this chapter you will learn about the effects of these powerful forces of nature.

Journal *Activity*

You and Your World   Have you ever visited the Grand Canyon or seen pictures of it? It is a remarkable place. In your journal, write a postcard to a friend describing a visit, real or imaginary, to the Grand Canyon. Try to capture in words the immense size of the canyon.

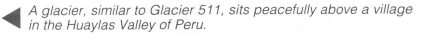

◀ *A glacier, similar to Glacier 511, sits peacefully above a village in the Huaylas Valley of Peru.*

6–1 Changing the Earth's Surface

Millions of years ago, the Colorado River flowed slowly across a broad flat area in present day Arizona. If you were to visit the area today, you would see a huge gorge called the Grand Canyon. The Grand Canyon was carved out of the Earth by **erosion** (ih-ROH-zhuhn). Erosion is the process by which weathered rock and soil particles are moved from one place to another. In Chapter 5 you learned that weathering is the breaking down of rocks and other materials on the Earth's surface. Erosion carries away the products of weathering.

Rocks and soil particles carried away by erosion are deposited in other places. Over time, these materials build up to create new landforms. The process by which sediments are laid down in new locations is called **deposition** (dehp-uh-ZIHSH-uhn). Both erosion and deposition change the shape of the Earth's surface. Erosion moves materials from place to place. Deposition builds new landforms. Weathering, erosion, and deposition form a cycle of forces that wear down and build up the Earth's surface.

Erosion can be caused by gravity, wind, running water, glaciers, and waves. These are the five agents of erosion. An agent of erosion is a material or force that moves sediments from place to place.

Figure 6–1 For millions of years, the Colorado River carved a huge gorge out of a once broad, flat area of the Earth's surface. Today, a small raft is dwarfed by the tall cliffs of the Grand Canyon.

6–1 Section Review

1. What are the five agents of erosion? How does erosion change the Earth's surface?
2. What is deposition? How does deposition change the surface of the Earth?

Critical Thinking—*Relating Concepts*
3. A girl using a garden hose to water a vegetable bed notices that a slight depression forms where the water hits the ground. She also notices that excess water running down a cement path is brown. Relate these observations to the formation of the Grand Canyon.

6–2 Gravity

Gravity pulls rocks and soil down slopes. The downhill movement of sediments caused by gravity is called **mass wasting.** Mass wasting can occur rapidly or slowly. In either case, sediments come to rest at the bottom of a slope in a formation called a talus slope. You have read about a talus slope in Chapter 5.

One example of rapid mass wasting is a landslide. A landslide is a tumbling of soil, rocks, and boulders down a slope. A landslide can be caused by an earthquake, a volcanic eruption, or the weakening of supporting rocks as a result of heavy rain. Once a landslide begins, it can move millions of tons of rocks down a slope and cause tremendous damage.

A mudflow is another example of rapid mass wasting. A mudflow usually occurs after a heavy rain. The rain mixes with the soil to form mud. The mud begins to slide downhill, picking up more soil and becoming thicker. A mudflow can move just about anything in its path—including boulders and houses.

Sometimes a huge block of rock will slide rapidly down a slope. This type of mass wasting is called slump. Slump occurs when rock resistant to weathering lies on a layer of weak or unstable rock. The underlying rock begins to slip down the slope, and the entire block of rock breaks off and slides downhill.

Guide for Reading

Focus on this question as you read.

▶ *How does gravity cause erosion?*

Figure 6–2 *Loose rocks can be moved down a hill by the force of gravity in a form of mass wasting known as a landslide (left). A mudslide (center) and a slump (right) are two other examples of earth movement due to gravity.*

Earthflows and soil creep are two examples of slow mass wasting. An earthflow usually occurs after a heavy rain. A mass of soil and plant life slowly slides down a slope. Soil creep is the slowest kind of mass wasting. Alternating periods of freezing and thawing, animal activity, or water movement disturb the soil particles. As the particles begin to move, gravity pulls them slowly downhill.

6–2 Section Review

1. How does gravity cause erosion?
2. What is rapid mass wasting? Give two examples.
3. What is slow mass wasting? Give two examples.

Critical Thinking—*Language Arts*
4. Why is mass wasting an appropriate term?

Guide for Reading

Focus on this question as you read.

▶ *Where does wind cause the greatest amount of erosion?*

6–3 Wind

Have you ever seen a person lose his or her hat to a brisk gust of wind? If so, you know that wind is a powerful force—often powerful enough to move materials from one place to another. Certain locations are more easily affected by wind erosion than others are. **Wind is the most active agent of erosion in deserts, in plowed fields, and on beaches.** In these places loose material is exposed at the Earth's surface. This loose material can easily be picked up and carried by the wind.

Types of Wind Erosion

Wind erodes the Earth's surface in two ways. Wind removes loose materials such as clay, silt, dust, and sand from the land. This type of wind erosion is called deflation (dih-FLAY-shuhn). Fine particles are carried many meters up into the air. Larger particles rise only a few centimeters. Do you know why?

As the wind blows, the larger particles roll or bounce along the ground. These particles slowly wear away exposed rocks. The particles often act like a sandblaster, cutting and polishing rocks. This type of wind erosion is called abrasion. In nature the rock particles worn away by abrasion are carried away by the wind. What effect can these particles have on other rock surfaces?

The amount of erosion caused by wind depends on the size of the particles being carried, the speed of the wind, and the length of time the wind blows. It also depends on the resistance of the rocks exposed to the wind.

In many desert regions wind erosion forms wind caves by wearing away less-resistant material. Sometimes wind erodes desert sands down to the depth where water is present. With water available on the surface, trees, shrubs, and grasses grow. Then a green, fertile area within a desert, called an oasis (oh-AY-suhs), forms.

Deposits by Wind

The amount of rock and soil particles carried by wind depends on the speed of the wind. The faster the wind blows, the more particles it can carry. The slower the wind blows, the fewer particles it can carry. As the speed of the wind decreases, the particles it can no longer carry are deposited.

DUNES In desert areas and along shorelines, windblown sand is often deposited near rocks and

Figure 6–3 *Wind erosion carved these beautiful caves in Sandstone Canyon, Arizona. In some places in a desert, wind erodes sand away to a depth where water is present. With water, plants are able to grow and eventually an oasis forms.*

Figure 6–4 *Formed by wind-blown sand, a dune on the shore of Lake Michigan is populated by a variety of plants. A dune formed by wind-blown sand in Death Valley shows no plant life. What accounts for this difference in the two dunes?*

Figure 6–5 *This loess deposit is a nearly vertical cliff of sand and silt. Does a loess deposit show any visible layers?*

bushes. Wind blowing over these deposits is slowed down. More sand is deposited. The mounds of sand continue to grow and to form **sand dunes.** A sand dune is a mound of sand deposited by wind. Sand dunes are very important features of a beach area. They protect the area on the side of the dune away from the ocean from further wind erosion. Small plants often grow on a sand dune. The roots and stems of these plants hold the sand in place. In this way the plants protect the dune from erosion. On some dunes, you may have seen signs cautioning you to avoid stepping on or removing plants. Can you now explain why these signs are important?

Sand dunes vary in size and in shape. Figure 6–6 shows how a sand dune forms. Notice that the side of the dune facing the wind has a gentle slope. Sand is carried up the gentle slope, or windward side, to the crest, or top of the dune. At the crest, the sand is dropped by the wind. The sand slides down the other side. This side of the dune, the slip face, has a steep slope.

As the wind blows, sand dunes move across the areas where they form. They move in the direction the wind is blowing. A sand dune moves by being eroded on one side and built up on the other side. Sometimes moving sand dunes cover buildings, farmlands, and trees.

LOESS Some fine particles of sand and silt are not deposited in dunes. Instead, they are deposited by the wind many kilometers from where they were picked up. When many layers of fine sand and silt are deposited in the same area, **loess** (LOH-ehs) is formed. Loess deposits are very fertile.

Deposits of loess are light in color and may be many meters thick. Loess deposits are found near the northern and central parts of the Mississippi River Valley. They are also found in northeast China.

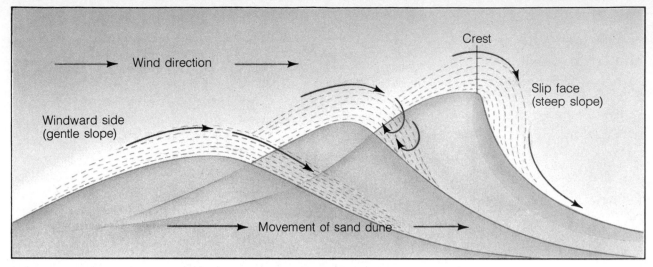

Figure 6–6 *A sand dune forms as material carried by the wind moves up the gentle slope, or windward side, of the dune and accumulates at the crest. Then this material moves down the steep slope, or slip face, of the dune and forms a series of layers. In this same way, a sand dune moves across the area where it forms. On what side of the dune does erosion take place? Deposition?*

Large dust storms in the Gobi desert in Asia have formed loess deposits hundreds of meters thick.

A windbreak is often used to decrease wind erosion and aid in wind deposition. A windbreak is a barrier that causes the wind to slow down. What happens when the wind slows down? When wind speed is decreased, the load carried by the wind is dropped. Fences are often used as windbreaks. So are plants. Consequently, many farmers surround their fields with bushes or trees to help stop wind erosion.

6–3 Section Review

1. Where is wind the most active agent of erosion?
2. How are deflation and abrasion different?
3. What are two kinds of deposits caused by wind?

Connection—*Ecology*
4. At certain beaches, you can often observe a short fence made of thin slats of vertical wood held together at the top and bottom by thin strands of wire. These fences are not tall enough or strong enough to make effective barriers to animals or people. They have an important function, however. Propose a hypothesis that explains what these fences are used for.

6–4 Running Water

From gently falling raindrops to rushing rivers, running water changes more of the Earth's surface than any other agent of erosion. **Running water is the major cause of erosion.**

Rivers, streams, and runoff are forms of running water. Runoff is water that flows over the Earth's surface, usually after a rainfall or a spring thaw. Runoff flows into streams and rivers.

Runoff and Erosion

When rain falls on the surface of the Earth, three things can happen to the water. The rain can evaporate, it can sink into the ground, or it can flow over the land surface as runoff.

When water moves across the Earth's surface as runoff, it picks up and carries particles of clay, sand, and gravel. Because of gravity, the water and sediments move downhill. As the water and sediments move downhill, they cut into the soil and form tiny grooves, called rills. As erosion continues, the rills become wider and deeper. Eventually, gullies form. Gullies act as channels for runoff. You may have seen gullies on slopes alongside highways. Where else might you see gullies caused by erosion?

The amount of runoff is affected by several factors. One factor is the amount of rainfall in an area. In areas with a high average rainfall, there is a lot of runoff. When there is a lot of runoff, there is a lot of erosion.

The amount of runoff is also affected by the amount of plant growth in an area. Plant roots hold soil particles in place. The soil absorbs some of the water. The plant roots also absorb some of the water. Areas with little plant growth have greater runoff and therefore greater erosion. Soil with little plant life can easily be washed away since there are few roots to hold the soil in place.

The shape of the land also affects the amount of runoff. Areas that have steep slopes have the greatest amount of runoff. On a steep slope the water moves too fast to soak into the ground. As the water

FIND OUT BY DOING

Running Water and Erosion

1. After a heavy rain, collect a sample of runoff in a clear plastic container.

2. Let the water stand for about 10 minutes.

3. Observe the bottom of the container for sediments carried by the runoff.

4. Collect and observe samples from several other areas.

Are there any differences in the samples? Was the runoff from one particular area carrying more sediments than the runoff from other areas? Explain your answer.

Figure 6–7 *Farmers often lose land to the forces of erosion. This gully was once a stream bed. What happened to the soil in this area?*

moves rapidly downhill, a lot of erosion takes place. If land surfaces have adequate plant life and are properly cared for, little erosion will occur. Why is it important to control runoff?

Streams and Erosion

Gullies formed by runoff are actually tiny stream valleys. When runoff from several gullies comes together, a larger stream forms.

Streams are important agents of erosion because they carry large amounts of sediments. The soil particles and rock materials carried by a stream are called the stream's **load.** Large and fast-moving streams can carry big loads.

Sediments in a stream's load are transported in different ways. Large, heavy sediments, such as pebbles and boulders, are pushed or rolled downstream. Lighter sediments, such as silt or mud, are picked up and carried along by the force of the moving water. Still other sediments, such as salts, dissolve in the stream water.

Streams cause erosion by abrasion. Sediments carried by streams constantly collide with rocks, chipping away pieces and wearing down the rocks.

Sometimes the layers of rocks beneath a stream are eroded by abrasion. If the stream flows first over hard rock layers and then over soft rock layers, a waterfall will form. This is because abrasion wears away the soft rocks faster than it does the hard rocks. In time, the level of the stream flowing over the soft rocks is lower than the level of the stream flowing over the hard rocks. A waterfall results.

FIND OUT BY
READING

The Good Earth

Although Pearl Buck was born in the United States, she spent a good part of her life in China. One of her novels, *The Good Earth,* describes the effects of river floods on the lives of people. You might enjoy reading this book, considered to be a classic by many people.

You might be interested to learn that Pearl Buck was also the first woman to win the Nobel prize for literature—a very great honor indeed.

Figure 6–8 *As abrasion wears away underlying rock layers unevenly, a waterfall forms.*

Development of a River System

As you have just read, runoff forms rills. Rills deepen and widen to form gullies. Gullies then join to form streams. Finally, streams join to form rivers. Rivers usually begin in mountains or hills. The downward pull of gravity gives them energy to cut away the land and form valleys. Rivers are important agents of erosion because they affect a large area.

The network of rills, gullies, streams, and rivers in an area is called a **drainage system.** You can compare the pattern of channels in a drainage system to the pattern of branches on a tree. The small twigs of a tree that grow from small branches are like the rills and gullies that join to form streams. The small branches are connected to larger branches just as the small streams flow into larger streams. These larger streams are called **tributaries** (TRIHB-yoo-tehr-eez). The tributaries flow into the main river in much the same way as the larger branches are joined to the trunk of the tree. The main river is like the tree trunk. In time the main river empties into another river, a lake, or an ocean at a place called the mouth of the river.

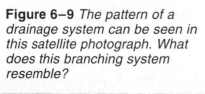

Figure 6–9 *The pattern of a drainage system can be seen in this satellite photograph. What does this branching system resemble?*

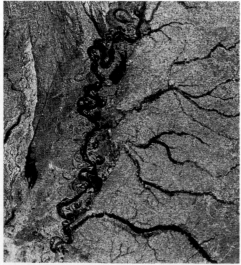

The area drained by a main river and its channels is called a **drainage basin.** The land that separates one drainage basin from another is called a divide. One of the largest divides is the Continental Divide, located about 80 kilometers west of Denver, Colorado. The Continental Divide is a continuous line that runs north and south the length of North America. West of the divide, all water eventually flows into the Pacific Ocean. East of the divide, all water eventually flows into the Atlantic Ocean.

A divide starts off as a wide area. But as the drainage system of a river develops, the divide becomes narrower. Sometimes a drainage system will cut through its divide and steal runoff from another drainage basin.

A drainage system grows larger by deepening its channels, widening its valleys, and adding more rills and gullies to its system. The river grows larger and faster, and the river valley grows deeper and wider. In time the river reaches a balance between the processes of erosion and deposition.

Life Cycle of a River

An **immature river,** or young river, is a river in an early stage of development. An immature river cuts a valley with steep sides into the Earth's surface. The valley is typically V-shaped, and the river covers almost the entire valley floor. The waters of an immature river flow very quickly over rocks, producing rapids. Waterfalls are also commonly found in immature rivers. These rivers erode the surrounding areas rapidly. What size particles do you think an immature river is able to carry?

A river that has been developing for many thousands of years is called a **mature river.** Because of continuous erosion, the rapids and waterfalls have largely disappeared. The river has also eroded much of the valley floor. The valley walls are far from the river itself. The floor of the valley is broad and flat. What shape do you think such a valley is described as having? The course of the river has also become curved and winding, forming loops called **meanders** (mee-AN-derz). The river has slowed down, so erosion has slowed down. What size particles do you think a mature river is able to carry?

Figure 6–10 *The Upper Bow River, in Banff National Park, Canada, is an example of an immature river (right). The Niobrara River in Nebraska is an example of a mature river (left). How are these two rivers different?*

Deposits by Rivers

A stream or river carries a large amount of sediments. In places where the stream or river slows down, sediments are deposited. Some of the larger sediments settle on the riverbed, or the bottom of the river channel. Some sediments are deposited along the river bank, or the side of the river. These deposits constantly change surrounding land areas.

Sediments are usually deposited on a river bank where a river bends, or curves. This is because the speed of a river decreases at a bend. Rivers tend to erode material on the outside of the curve and deposit it on the inside. The outside of the curve receives the full impact of the current. The water on the inside of a river bend moves more slowly.

OXBOW LAKES   Sometimes the meanders of a river form large, U-shaped bends. Erosion and deposition along such bends can cut these bends off from the river. Deposited sediments dam up the ends of the meander. A small lake called an **oxbow lake** is formed. An oxbow lake is separated from the river. Figure 6–11 shows how an oxbow lake forms.

ALLUVIAL FANS   When a river leaves the mountains and runs out onto a plain, its speed decreases. Nearly all the sediments the river is carrying are dropped. They build up to form an **alluvial fan.** The sediments spread out from the river channel in a fanlike shape.

DELTAS   Large amounts of sediments deposited at the mouth of a large river that flows into a lake or an ocean form a **delta.** A delta forms because the river's speed decreases as it runs into the body of

Figure 6–11 *An oxbow lake is often formed when a meander is cut off from the rest of the river. What type of river might have oxbow lakes along its course?*

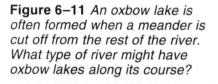
Meandering river
1

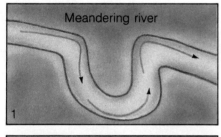
Narrowing neck
2

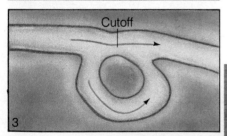
Cutoff
3

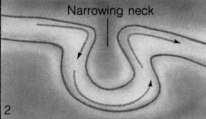
Deposited sediment
Oxbow lake
4

standing water. The river cannot carry as much material when it is moving slowly. So it deposits much of the sediments. Sediments build up above the river's water level. What river delta is closest to where you live?

FLOOD PLAINS AND LEVEES On both sides of a mature river or stream, flat areas called **flood plains** form. After heavy rains or spring thaws, the river overflows its banks and covers the flood plain. Sediments are deposited on the plain. Repeated flooding causes sediments to build up. Flood plains have fertile soil. For example, the flood plains on either side of the Mississippi River are very fertile areas as a result of the periodic flooding of the river. What might be a good use for these areas?

Sediments deposited on a flood plain usually consist of fine particles. The larger particles, which settle first, are deposited along the sides of the river. These particles form a ridgelike deposit called a **levee** (LEHV-ee).

Figure 6–12 *An alluvial fan forms when a river leaves the mountains and slows down as it runs out onto a plain (right). As a large river flows into a lake or ocean, its speed decreases and it deposits large amounts of sediments. These deposits form a delta (left).*

6–4 Section Review

1. What is the major cause of erosion?
2. What factors affect the amount of runoff?
3. What is a drainage system? A drainage basin?
4. Compare an immature river to a mature river.
5. How are deltas and flood plains formed?

Connection—*Ecology*

6. Flood plains have fertile soil and can produce good crops. However, flood plains might not be good places to build houses. Explain why.

6–5 Glaciers

A **glacier** (GLAY-shuhr) is a large mass of moving ice and snow. Glaciers form where there are many large snowfalls and the temperatures remain very cold. Some glaciers form in high mountains where the snow that falls in the winter does not completely melt in the summer. The snow builds up over the years and gradually turns to ice. These glaciers move very slowly through valleys down the mountains. These glaciers are called valley glaciers.

Other glaciers form in the polar regions of the world. Some of these glaciers are huge sheets of ice called continental glaciers or icecaps. They often cover millions of square kilometers. See Figure 6–13. What areas of the Earth do you think are covered with continental glaciers?

Glacial Ice and Erosion

A glacier is one of the most powerful agents of erosion. **Glacial ice erodes by abrasion and by plucking away at the rock beneath it.**

As a glacier moves through a valley, rocks, gravel, and silt are carried along and pushed in front of it. Gravel and silt carried by a glacier are called glacial debris. Other rocks and debris are frozen into the ice at the bottom of the glacier. Still more rocks and debris are loosened from the valley walls as the glacier scrapes against them.

A glacier may carry along large boulders as well as smaller particles of rocks. These make up the

Figure 6–13 *Valley glaciers are long, narrow sheets of ice that move down steep mountain slopes (left). Continental glaciers are huge sheets of ice that cover vast areas of the Earth's polar regions (right). What continent is covered almost entirely by a glacier?*

glacier's load. The load of a glacier helps to wear down the land surface by grinding and polishing the rock it passes over. Erosion caused by glaciers is similar to erosion caused by streams and rivers in that glacial erosion changes V-shaped mountain valleys into U-shaped mountain valleys.

During the Ice Age, huge icecaps covered a large part of North America. The Rocky Mountains, the mountains of New England, and many of the states in the Northeast and Midwest were at one time covered by glaciers. Glacial erosion caused many of the surface features that are present in these areas. For example, the Great Lakes were formed by glaciers.

Deposits by Glaciers

When the lower end of a glacier reaches a warm area, the ice at the front begins to melt. The glacier continues to move forward, but it may be melting so rapidly at the front that it appears to be moving backward. Such a glacier is said to be retreating. As it retreats, rocks and debris are deposited.

Rocks and debris deposited directly by a glacier are called **till.** Till is a mixture of material that varies in size from large boulders to very fine clay particles. Till is not sorted out by the action of running water. In other words, the material in till is not separated into layers according to its size.

Other glacial deposits are sorted out by running water from melting glaciers. The coarse and fine materials are separated into layers. Both sorted and unsorted materials are found in different features of the land formed by glaciers.

MORAINES When a glacier melts and retreats, it leaves behind till. The till forms a ridge called a **moraine.** There are different types of moraines. Till deposited at the front end of a glacier is called a terminal moraine. Till deposited along the sides of a glacier is called a lateral moraine.

Scientists can find out about glaciers that have melted by studying moraines. The rocks found in a moraine are evidence of where the glacier formed. Rocks can be carried great distances by glaciers. The position of a terminal moraine indicates how far the glacier advanced before retreating.

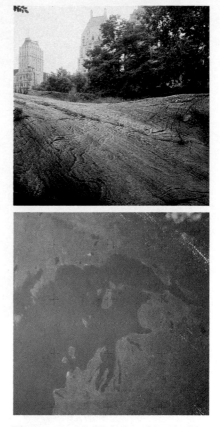

Figure 6–14 *This boulder in New York City's Central Park shows grooves etched by rocks carried along by retreating glaciers. You might be surprised to learn that much of New York City was covered by a glacier during the last Ice Age. The Great Lakes were also formed by the action of glaciers.*

Figure 6–15 *Till left behind when a glacier melts and retreats forms ridges called moraines. Where is a lateral moraine located? A terminal moraine?*

DRUMLINS   A **drumlin** is an oval-shaped mound of till. Its tip points in the direction that the glacier was moving. Scientists believe that drumlins are formed as deposits of till are rounded by the glacial ice.

MELTWATER DEPOSITS   When valley glaciers stop advancing, melting ice forms streams that flow out from the glacier. These streams are called **meltwater** streams. The meltwater carries away sand and gravel. The sand and gravel sediments are deposited along the meltwater stream in long trainlike deposits called valley trains. The meltwater may also form small lakes and ponds near the glacier. Many present-day rivers were originally meltwater streams.

Sediments deposited by rivers of glacial meltwater form areas called **outwash plains.** Outwash plains are fan-shaped and form in front of terminal moraines. Outwash plains are very fertile land areas. Today many farms can be found in outwash plains.

ICEBERG DEPOSITS   Valley glaciers and continental glaciers sometimes reach the sea. When this happens, the glaciers form cliffs of ice and snow. Parts of the glaciers break off and drift into the sea. These glacial parts are called **icebergs.** The continental glaciers of Greenland and Antarctica are the major sources of icebergs.

Figure 6–16 *What appear to be gently rolling hills are actually glacial deposits called drumlins. A drumlin is an oval-shaped mound of till. What is till?*

Icebergs may contain rocks and debris picked up from the land. As the icebergs melt, the rocks and debris are deposited on the ocean floor. These sediments are often found thousands of kilometers from their source.

GLACIAL LAKES Glaciers created many of the lakes in the United States. The Finger Lakes in New York, the Great Lakes, and many smaller lakes were formed by glaciers. Do you know of any other lakes that were formed by glaciers?

Figure 6–17 *Icebergs form when chunks of glacial ice break off and drift into the sea. Often icebergs are a danger to ships. A kettle pond forms when a block of glacial ice, surrounded by or covered with sediments, melts and leaves a hole that fills with water. Kettle ponds can be seen in Yosemite National Park.*

Figure 6–18 *The various land features formed by glacial deposits are shown in this diagram. What are some of these features?*

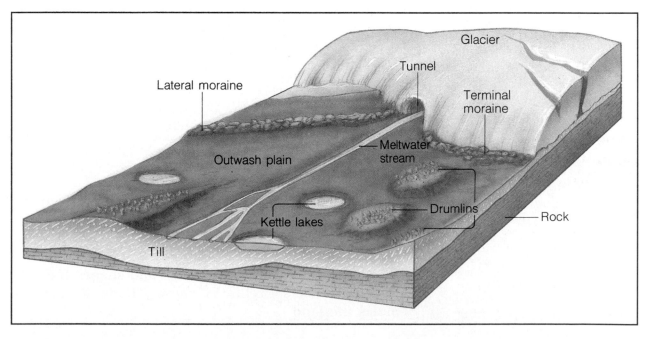

FIND OUT BY DOING

Glacial Erosion

1. Cover a sheet of cardboard with a layer of clay 1 centimeter thick.

2. Rub some sand on top of the clay.

3. Slide an ice cube slowly along a path in the sand. Then hold the ice cube in one place and allow some of it to melt.

Describe the appearance of the sand after the ice cube has slid over it. What do you notice about the ice cube? What happened in the place where you held the cube?

■ How does this activity relate to the erosion processes of glaciers?

Glaciers can form lakes in two ways. Glacial till or deposits of sorted sediments from meltwater sometimes pile up in low-lying river channels and other areas. These deposits keep water from flowing away from the area. The land areas fill with water, and lakes are formed.

Sometimes huge blocks of glacial ice are left behind by a glacier. The ice blocks are surrounded by or covered with sediments deposited by the glacier. When the ice melts, it leaves a depression, or hole, in the ground. The depression fills with water and forms a lake. Lakes formed in this way are called **kettle lakes.** Kettle lakes are usually round and very deep.

6–5 Section Review

1. How does a glacier erode the Earth's surface?
2. Compare a valley glacier and a continental glacier.
3. What is till? A moraine? A drumlin?
4. What are two meltwater deposits?
5. How are glacial lakes formed?

Critical Thinking—*Applying Concepts*
6. While walking in a valley in a national park located near a snow-capped mountain range, Betty noticed large piles of rocks, boulders, sand, and fine clay particles all mixed together. The piles were unlike the small rocks she had previously noticed. Propose a theory to explain Betty's observations.

Guide for Reading

Focus on this question as you read.

▶ How do waves affect a shoreline?

6–6 Waves

If you have ever been to an ocean beach, you are probably familiar with waves. Waves are caused by winds, by tides, and sometimes even by earthquakes. Waves can be extremely powerful. **The powerful force of waves constantly erodes and shapes the shoreline.** The shoreline is where a body of water meets the land.

Waves and Erosion

Waves cause erosion in several ways. As ocean waves reach shallow water near the shore, they begin to break. As the breaking waves hit the shoreline, their force knocks fragments off existing rock formations. Waves also carry small rocks and sand. The force of the small rocks and sand particles hitting other rocks on the shoreline chips off fragments. What kind of weathering is taking place in these two types of wave erosion?

Another way waves cause erosion is by forcing water into cracks in the rocks at the shoreline. The water causes pressure to build up in the cracks. Over time, the cracks become larger, and the pressure breaks the rocks. Because some rocks dissolve in salt water, the chemical action of salt water also breaks down rocks.

Erosion at the shoreline can occur at different rates. Various conditions cause these different rates. The size and force of the waves hitting the shoreline have an effect on the rate of erosion. Under normal conditions, waves may erode the shoreline at a rate of 1 to 1.5 meters per year. During storms, however, wave action is increased. Larger waves hit the shoreline with greater force. The rate of shoreline erosion may increase to 25 meters in one day. The type of rock that makes up the shoreline also affects the rate of erosion. Some rocks do not erode as quickly as others. How might wave erosion differ along ocean shores and lake shores?

Figure 6–19 *The powerful force of waves constantly erodes rocks and reshapes the shoreline. Why are people cautioned about building homes near the shoreline?*

Figure 6–20 *Sea stacks are the remains of a cliff that was eroded away by waves. A sea cave is a hollowed-out portion of a sea cliff.*

SEA CLIFFS AND TERRACES   Wave erosion forms a variety of features along a shoreline. Erosion by waves sometimes produces steep faces of rock called **sea cliffs.** Over a long period of time the bottom of a sea cliff may be worn away by wave action. Overhanging rocks may break off the top of the cliff and fall into the sea. Waves will then grind the rocks into sand and silt.

As the sea cliff continues to be eroded, the buildup of rocks, sand, and silt forms a flat platform at the base of the cliff. This flat platform is called a **terrace.** As waves move across the terrace, they are slowed down. They strike the cliff with less force. Terraces slow down erosion of sea cliffs.

SEA STACKS AND CAVES   As waves erode a sea cliff, columns of resistant rock may be left standing. These columns are called **sea stacks.** Sometimes part of a sea cliff is made of less-resistant rock. When wave action erodes this rock, a cave is formed. A **sea cave** is a hollowed out portion of a sea cliff.

Deposits by Waves

Waves carry large amounts of sand, rock particles, and pieces of shells. At some point waves deposit the material they carry. Sand and other sediments carried away from one part of the shoreline by waves may be deposited elsewhere on the shoreline. The shape of the shoreline is always changing.

BEACHES   Eroded rock particles deposited on the shoreline form beaches. Beaches may consist of fine sand or of large pebbles. Some beach materials come directly from the erosion of nearby areas of the shoreline. Other beach materials can come from rivers that carry sediments from inland areas to the sea. Waves transport the sediments from the mouths of rivers to different parts of the shoreline.

The type of material found on a beach varies according to its source. The color of the sand provides a clue to its origin. Beaches along the Atlantic coast have white sand. White sand usually consists of quartz material that originated in the eastern part of the United States. For example, most of the white sand on the Atlantic coast of Florida came from the erosion of the southern Appalachian Mountains. On Hawaii and other islands in the Pacific, some sand is black. This black sand comes from broken fragments of dark, volcanic rocks. Still other beaches may have deposits of shell fragments and coral skeletons.

SAND BARS AND SPITS Waves do not usually move straight into the shore. Instead, they approach the shore at an angle. The water is then turned so it runs parallel to the shoreline. The movement of water parallel to a shoreline is called a **longshore current.**

If the shoreline bends or curves, material carried by waves in a longshore current is deposited in open water. A long, underwater ridge of sand called a **sand bar** forms. If the sand bar is connected to the curving shoreline, it is called a **spit.**

Sometimes large sand bars are formed during the winter. At this time of year waves are large and carry more material away from the beaches. This material is deposited offshore. What do you think happens during the summer?

Figure 6–21 *The sand found on a beach varies according to its source. The color of sand is a clue to its origin and composition. What is the likely origin of white sand? Black sand? Pink sand?*

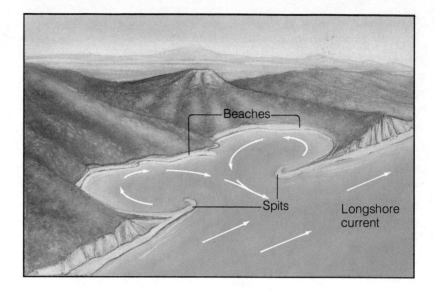

Beaches
Spits
Longshore current

The Shape of a Shoreline

The shape of a shoreline often results from changes in the level of the sea. If the sea level drops, the resulting shoreline has many sea cliffs and terraces. The drop in sea level exposes new areas of shore to wave erosion, which forms many sea cliffs and terraces.

If the sea level rises, the resulting shoreline has many bays and harbors. The rise in sea level floods streams and small rivers, forming bays and harbors.

FIND OUT BY
WRITING

What Causes Erosion and Deposition?

In a 300-word essay, describe how the processes of erosion and deposition occur. Use the following words in your essay.

continental glacier
valley glacier
terminal moraine
oxbow lake
sea stack
spits
loess
slip face

6–6 Section Review

1. How do waves affect a shoreline?
2. What is a sea cliff? A sea stack?
3. Why do different beaches have different colored sand?
4. How does a longshore current form sand bars and spits?

Connection—*Ecology*
5. Many people have built houses on beaches. The view of the ocean causes land along the shore to be highly valued. However, many scientists warn against building a house on the beach front. Why do you think the scientists warn against this?

Nature's Gifts From the Nile

Life on Earth often forms webs of great complexity. In this chapter, you have read about the fertility of lands that form a river's flood plains. These lands, renewed by periodic deposits of silt and minerals, are part of the river's bounty of life. The crops produced in fertile flood plains provide food and fibers for millions of people who often live many, many kilometers from the river's banks.

The Nile River performed this life-giving role in ages past. Heavy rains caused the Nile to flood every year. As the river's waters overspilled the banks, land in the flood plains was inundated. Deposits carried by the river were left behind as the water receded. These deposits enhanced the soil's fertility—Egypt could produce enough food to feed its people.

Today progress and technology have altered life along the Nile. The Aswan Dam, completed in 1971, was viewed with hope and promise. It was thought that the dam would control the annual flooding of the Nile, as well as generate enough electricity to power industrial plants that would provide jobs for millions of Egypt's inhabitants. It did all that. But it also altered the web of life that had existed almost unchanged for thousands of years along the river.

Today farmers along the Nile cannot depend on the annual flooding of the Nile to enrich their soil. They must add artificial fertilizers to provide food for their crops. Some scientists have calculated that the power produced by the dam today equals the power needed to make fertilizers for the area's crops. In this case, nature might have known best. The Nile River is controlled by modern technology, and its annual floodings are no more. However, one must wonder if the lives of those living in the area have been improved very much, if at all.

Laboratory Investigation

Observing Erosion and Deposition in a Model Stream

Problem

How is a stream's ability to erode and deposit materials affected by a change in its flow?

Materials *(per group)*

lab table
support, such as books
stream pan (2 cm x 50 cm x 8–10 cm)
sand
2 buckets
2 25-cm lengths of rubber tubing (1 cm in diameter)
screw clamp
food coloring or ink

Procedure

1. Set up a stream table similar to the one shown in the illustration.

2. Raise one end of the large pan slightly, so that the pan forms a very low angle with the table. To start the water flowing, siphon the water out of the bucket. Use the screw clamp to set the water flow at a low volume.

3. As the water runs to the end of the pan, observe and record the changes that occur on the land surface, on the lake, and on the stream itself. Note any deposition features that may form. A drop of food coloring or ink can help to reveal patterns of change.

4. Next, change the slope of the stream, making it steep by increasing the angle between the pan and the table. Observe and record the effects of this change.

5. Now increase the stream's volume by opening the screw clamp or by pouring water down the stream table. Observe and record the effects of this change.

Observations

1. What, if any, deposition features formed?

2. What evidence of erosion did you observe?

3. What changes in the stream occurred when you increased the steepness of the slope of your stream table? When you increased the volume of water?

Analysis and Conclusions

1. What effects does an increase in the speed at which the stream flows have on the processes of erosion and deposition? An increase in stream volume?

2. Why do you think old rivers meander?

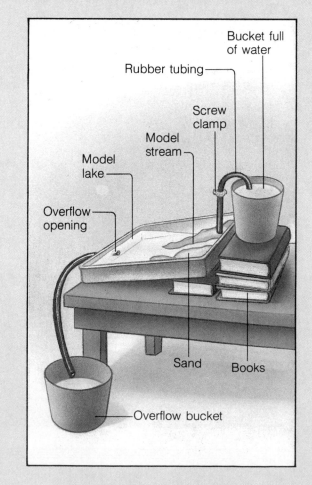

Summarizing Key Concepts

6–1 Changing the Earth's Surface

▲ Erosion is the process by which weathered rock and soil particles are moved from one place to another.

▲ Deposition is the process by which sediments are laid down in new locations.

▲ The five agents of erosion are gravity, wind, running water, glaciers, and waves.

6–2 Gravity

▲ The downhill movement of sediments caused by gravity is called mass wasting.

6–3 Wind

▲ Wind erodes by deflation and abrasion.

▲ Sand dunes and loess are wind deposits.

6–4 Running Water

▲ Running water in the form of rivers, streams, and runoff is the major agent of erosion.

▲ The network of rills, gullies, streams, and rivers in an area is called a drainage system.

▲ Deposits by rivers include oxbow lakes, alluvial fans, deltas, flood plains, and levees.

6–5 Glaciers

▲ A glacier is a large mass of moving ice and snow. Two types of glaciers are valley glaciers and continental glaciers.

▲ Rocks and debris deposited directly by a glacier are called till.

▲ Other glacial deposits include moraines, drumlins, meltwater streams, outwash plains, icebergs, and lakes.

6–6 Waves

▲ Waves erode and shape the shoreline.

▲ Wave erosion forms sea cliffs, terraces, sea stacks, and sea caves.

▲ Deposits by waves include beaches, sand bars, and spits.

Reviewing Key Terms

Define each term in a complete sentence.

6–1 Changing the Earth's Surface
erosion
deposition

6–2 Gravity
mass wasting

6–3 Wind
sand dune
loess

6–4 Running Water
load
drainage
 system
tributary
drainage basin
immature river
mature river
meander
oxbow lake
alluvial fan
delta
flood plain
levee

6–5 Glaciers
glacier
till
moraine
drumlin
meltwater
outwash plain
iceberg
kettle lake

6–6 Waves
sea cliff
terrace
sea stack
sea cave
longshore
 current
sand bar
spit

Chapter Review

Content Review

Multiple Choice

Choose the letter of the answer that best completes each statement.

1. The process by which sediments are laid down in new locations is called
   a. erosion.
   b. deposition.
   c. abrasion.
   d. mass wasting.
2. Two examples of rapid mass wasting are
   a. slump and soil creep.
   b. landslides and earthflows.
   c. soil creep and earthflows.
   d. landslides and slump.
3. Layers of fine sand and silt deposited in the same area by wind are called
   a. loess.
   b. dunes.
   c. terraces.
   d. till.
4. The network of rills, gullies, and streams that forms a river is called a
   a. drainage basin.
   b. tributary.
   c. levee.
   d. drainage system.
5. Rich, fertile soil deposited on the sides of a river as it overflows forms flat areas called
   a. terraces.
   b. sand bars.
   c. flood plains.
   d. valley trains.
6. A ridge of till deposited as a glacier melts and retreats is called a
   a. moraine.
   b. terrace.
   c. levee.
   d. flood plain.
7. Glacial meltwater forms very fertile deposits of sediments called
   a. flood plains.
   b. outwash plains.
   c. kettle lakes.
   d. drumlins.
8. Columns of resistant rock left as waves erode sea cliffs are called
   a. spits.
   b. sea stacks.
   c. terraces.
   d. sand bars.
9. A sand bar connected to a curving shoreline is called a
   a. terrace.
   b. sea stack.
   c. spit.
   d. drumlin.
10. A shoreline that has many sea cliffs and terraces may indicate that the sea level has
    a. dropped.
    b. risen.
    c. remained constant.
    d. reversed direction.

True or False

If the statement is true, write "true." If it is false, change the underlined word or words to make the statement true.

1. The downhill movements of sediments is called <u>mass wasting</u>.
2. The most active agent of erosion in deserts and on beaches is <u>waves</u>.
3. When wind or water moves slowly, the amount of particles it can carry <u>increases</u>.
4. Areas with little plant growth have <u>more</u> erosion than areas with lots of plant growth.
5. A large deposit of sediment at the mouth of a river is called a <u>levee</u>.
6. Rocks and debris deposited directly by a glacier are called <u>till</u>.
7. Parts of glacial ice that break off and drift into the sea are called <u>drumlins</u>.

Concept Mapping

Complete the following concept map for Section 6–1. Refer to pages J6–J7 to construct a concept map for the entire chapter.

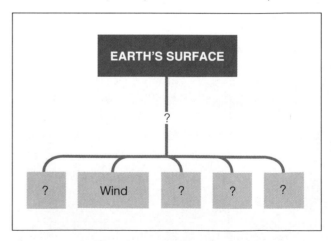

Concept Mastery

Discuss each of the following in a brief paragraph.

1. Explain why the rate of erosion along a shoreline increases during a storm.
2. Explain how both erosion and deposition occur at the same time in the formation of sand dunes.
3. What can scientists learn about glaciers by studying moraines?
4. List several agents of erosion that might affect land areas in a large city. Compare these agents with ones that might affect land areas in the country. Explain why different agents work in different areas.
5. Describe the formation of a waterfall. What role does water play?
6. Explain why farmland near rivers is often very productive.
7. Dams are usually built across rivers and streams. If the dam is large enough, a huge lake may form behind it. In what ways does a dam slow down erosion?
8. Continental glaciers may cause problems in areas that are far away from the site of the glacier. What kind of dangers can continental glaciers pose?
9. Wind erosion in a desert area is usually harmful. In one instance, however, it can be helpful. Explain how wind erosion in the desert can be helpful.

Critical Thinking and Problem Solving

Use the skills you have developed in this chapter to answer each of the following.

1. **Sequencing events** The following steps are stages in the formation of a river system from the time rain falls to the Earth to the time a steadily flowing river forms. The steps, however, are not in order. Read the steps and place them in the proper order.
   a. Runoff from several slopes collects in low places.
   b. Rain falls to the Earth's surface.
   c. Water tumbles in broad sheets.
   d. Branch gullies develop and then become tributaries.
   e. A gully is formed.
   f. A V-shaped valley with streams, waterfalls, and rapids forms.
   g. Erosion lengthens the gullies.
   h. The gully gets larger and collects more water.
2. **Relating concepts** Use glaciers as an example to explain how the erosion of a land area usually involves more than one agent of erosion.
3. **Making inferences** Why would a flood plain be characteristic of a mature river valley and not of an immature river valley?

4. **Applying concepts** What are two ways in which people cause erosion? What are two ways in which people can prevent erosion?
5. **Making diagrams** Make a diagram to show how an immature and a mature river would look in a photograph taken from a high-flying plane. How would each river look in a topographic map?
6. **Using the writing process** In order to protect shorelines, a proposal has been made to prohibit the construction of homes near beach dunes. Write a letter to your governor explaining your views.

SCIENCE GAZETTE

SARA BISEL UNCOVERS THE PAST WITH

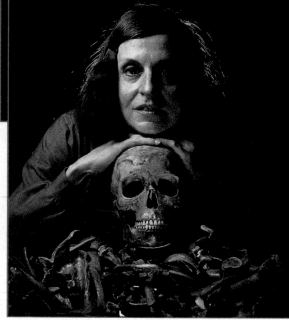

ANCIENT BONES

You probably know a bone when you see one. And you might even be able to tell the difference between a chicken bone and a steak bone. But if you saw a pile of bones, you probably couldn't tell much more about them. Dr. Sara Bisel is different. She studies bones to reveal a story within the bones—a story of ancient times. Dr. Bisel is an anthropologist, a person who studies the physical characteristics and cultures of people who lived in the past. She has studied chemistry, nutrition, and art. All of these fields help her in her work with bones.

Today, Sara Bisel works in Italy. There she studies the remains of a great disaster that occurred almost two thousand years ago. On August 24, AD 79, Mount Vesuvius, a volcano in southern Italy, erupted. For many people living near the volcano, this day was their last.

Summarizing Key Concepts

6–1 Changing the Earth's Surface

▲ Erosion is the process by which weathered rock and soil particles are moved from one place to another.

▲ Deposition is the process by which sediments are laid down in new locations.

▲ The five agents of erosion are gravity, wind, running water, glaciers, and waves.

6–2 Gravity

▲ The downhill movement of sediments caused by gravity is called mass wasting.

6–3 Wind

▲ Wind erodes by deflation and abrasion.

▲ Sand dunes and loess are wind deposits.

6–4 Running Water

▲ Running water in the form of rivers, streams, and runoff is the major agent of erosion.

▲ The network of rills, gullies, streams, and rivers in an area is called a drainage system.

▲ Deposits by rivers include oxbow lakes, alluvial fans, deltas, flood plains, and levees.

6–5 Glaciers

▲ A glacier is a large mass of moving ice and snow. Two types of glaciers are valley glaciers and continental glaciers.

▲ Rocks and debris deposited directly by a glacier are called till.

▲ Other glacial deposits include moraines, drumlins, meltwater streams, outwash plains, icebergs, and lakes.

6–6 Waves

▲ Waves erode and shape the shoreline.

▲ Wave erosion forms sea cliffs, terraces, sea stacks, and sea caves.

▲ Deposits by waves include beaches, sand bars, and spits.

Reviewing Key Terms

Define each term in a complete sentence.

6–1 Changing the Earth's Surface
erosion
deposition

6–2 Gravity
mass wasting

6–3 Wind
sand dune
loess

6–4 Running Water
load
drainage
  system
tributary
drainage basin
immature river
mature river
meander
oxbow lake
alluvial fan
delta
flood plain
levee

6–5 Glaciers
glacier
till
moraine
drumlin
meltwater
outwash plain
iceberg
kettle lake

6–6 Waves
sea cliff
terrace
sea stack
sea cave
longshore
  current
sand bar
spit

Chapter Review

Content Review

Multiple Choice

Choose the letter of the answer that best completes each statement.

1. The process by which sediments are laid down in new locations is called
   a. erosion. c. abrasion.
   b. deposition. d. mass wasting.
2. Two examples of rapid mass wasting are
   a. slump and soil creep.
   b. landslides and earthflows.
   c. soil creep and earthflows.
   d. landslides and slump.
3. Layers of fine sand and silt deposited in the same area by wind are called
   a. loess. c. terraces.
   b. dunes. d. till.
4. The network of rills, gullies, and streams that forms a river is called a
   a. drainage basin. c. levee.
   b. tributary. d. drainage system.
5. Rich, fertile soil deposited on the sides of a river as it overflows forms flat areas called
   a. terraces. c. flood plains.
   b. sand bars. d. valley trains.

6. A ridge of till deposited as a glacier melts and retreats is called a
   a. moraine. c. levee.
   b. terrace. d. flood plain.
7. Glacial meltwater forms very fertile deposits of sediments called
   a. flood plains. c. kettle lakes.
   b. outwash plains. d. drumlins.
8. Columns of resistant rock left as waves erode sea cliffs are called
   a. spits. c. terraces.
   b. sea stacks. d. sand bars.
9. A sand bar connected to a curving shoreline is called a
   a. terrace. c. spit.
   b. sea stack. d. drumlin.
10. A shoreline that has many sea cliffs and terraces may indicate that the sea level has
    a. dropped. c. remained constant.
    b. risen. d. reversed direction.

True or False

If the statement is true, write "true." If it is false, change the underlined word or words to make the statement true.

1. The downhill movements of sediments is called <u>mass wasting</u>.
2. The most active agent of erosion in deserts and on beaches is <u>waves</u>.
3. When wind or water moves slowly, the amount of particles it can carry <u>increases</u>.
4. Areas with little plant growth have <u>more</u> erosion than areas with lots of plant growth.
5. A large deposit of sediment at the mouth of a river is called a <u>levee</u>.
6. Rocks and debris deposited directly by a glacier are called <u>till</u>.
7. Parts of glacial ice that break off and drift into the sea are called <u>drumlins</u>.

Concept Mapping

Complete the following concept map for Section 6–1. Refer to pages J6–J7 to construct a concept map for the entire chapter.

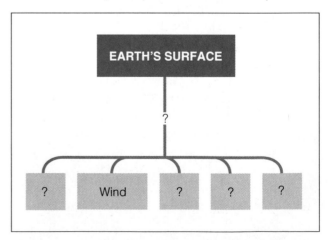

Herculaneum, a busy port city on the Bay of Naples, was located at the base of the volcano. The people of Herculaneum fished in the surrounding waters. They stored their fishing boats in stone huts on the beach. In one of the stone huts Sara Bisel made her most important discovery—not boats, but the remains of people who perished during the eruption of Mount Vesuvius. Although these remains are now only silent witnesses to a dreadful event, they tell a story to Sara Bisel.

▲ "Who says dead men don't talk?" From bones such as these, Dr. Bisel is reconstructing the lives of people buried during the eruption of Mount Vesuvius in AD 79.

"Who says dead men don't talk?" Dr. Bisel asks. "These bones will have a lot to say about who these people were and how they lived." For Dr. Bisel uncovers more than bones in her work. She tries to bring the lives of ancient people into focus.

In 1982 Dr. Bisel began to reconstruct the lives of people who hid in the boat shed during the eruption of Mount Vesuvius. That eruption was followed by an avalanche that buried the dead under thirty meters of lava and mud. This volcanic covering sealed the bones from the air. The mud hardened and preserved the skeletons.

Near the boat shed, Dr. Bisel found the remains of a woman she calls Portia. In examining Portia's badly crushed skull, Dr. Bisel concluded that Portia fell from a great height during the eruption. By measuring one of Portia's leg bones, Dr. Bisel was able to determine Portia's height. The condition of the bones also told Dr. Bisel about the kind of life Portia lived. For example, Dr. Bisel analyzed Portia's bones with special chemical tests. These tests could tell if Portia was well nourished and if she had any diseases. The shape and texture of the bones could tell what Portia did for a living. Ridges and rough spots on the arm bones indicated to Dr. Bisel the way in which Portia used her arm muscles. "I think she was a weaver."

Sara Bisel works carefully, loosening the fragile bones from their stony resting place. If the bones are treated roughly, they can break as easily as eggshells. She washes each bone and dips it into a liquid plastic solution to preserve it. Next she stores the bones in special yellow plastic boxes. To date, Dr. Bisel has collected the bones of 48 men, 38 women, and 25 children.

Putting the pieces of a skull together requires artistic skills as well as scientific knowledge. Sara Bisel is an expert at solving these complex, three-dimensional puzzles. "Just look at her profile and that delicate nose," Dr. Bisel exclaimed excitedly about Portia's reconstructed skull. "In your mind's eye, spread a little flesh over these bones. She was lovely!"

In one family, Dr. Bisel found four men, three women, and five children. One of the children was very young, only about seven months old the day of the eruption. Because the baby wore jewelry, Dr. Bisel thinks this family was wealthy.

Dr. Bisel, who works six days a week, truly enjoys her interesting job. She takes great delight in reconstructing the skeletons and discovering the stories they silently tell.

WASTING TIME:
The Nuclear Clock Ticks Down

Today, nuclear power plants are producing more than energy. They are producing a potentially deadly form of garbage: nuclear wastes!

By the year 2000, there will be enough nuclear garbage to fill a giant box about 40 meters on each side. Such a "box" would not be much larger than a 13-story building on a square city block. If there will be no more waste than this, what's the grave danger? Why all the fuss? The answer, in a single word, is radiation!

INVISIBLE DANGER

Radiation is invisible energy. And nuclear radiation is *powerful* invisible energy. It is so powerful, in fact, that even small doses over a period of time can permanently harm, or even kill, living things.

Substances such as uranium and plutonium are common fuels for nuclear power plants. Like other fuels, these substances

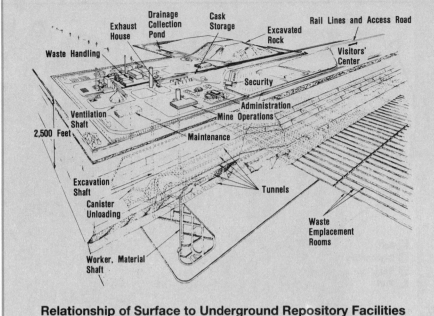

Relationship of Surface to Underground Repository Facilities

leave behind waste materials when they are used. But these wastes are not at all like the ashes that are the waste products of burning wood. Ashes are harmless. Nuclear wastes are extremely hazardous. The deadly radiation they give off can penetrate most ordinary substances. And this radiation can last for hundreds of thousands of years. So the disposal of nuclear wastes, even the smallest amount, is a giant problem.

Obviously, nuclear wastes cannot be disposed of like ordinary garbage. And they cannot be kept in giant containers, either. So how and where can they be safely stored? Scientists and engineers are trying to answer this question. But they cannot take forever to find a solution. For the wastes are piling up. Over the next few years, special tanks located near nuclear power plants will serve as temporary storehouses. But what is needed is a permanent home for these hazardous materials.

SPACE-BOUND GARBAGE

If we cannot find a place on Earth to get rid of nuclear garbage, why not send it into space? Rockets loaded with nuclear wastes could be launched into orbit between the Earth and Venus. Traveling at the right speeds, the rockets could stay in orbit for a million years or more without bumping into either planet. By that time, the nuclear wastes would have become harmless.

Critics of this idea point to its cost and potential danger. An accident during rocket launch could harm thousands of people. These critics believe that the solution is not in the stars but on Earth. Only where can these nuclear burying grounds be found?

▲ Storage of nuclear wastes requires a complex network of facilities. Here you see an artist's concept of the surface and underground features of a disposal site mined out of rock.

DOWN-TO-EARTH ALTERNATIVES

The Antarctic ice sheet is more than 2500 meters thick in some places. Could nuclear wastes be buried under this huge, frozen blanket? No, according to some critics of this idea. Not enough is known about the behavior of ice sheets. And what is known is not comforting. For example, ice sheets move rapidly about every 10,000 years. Their movement might allow the wastes to get loose. In addition, nuclear wastes produce a tremendous amount of heat—enough heat, in fact, to melt the ice. Where the ice melted, nuclear radiation might leak out into the oceans and air.

If not the Antarctic ice sheet, then how about a nuclear cemetery under the ocean floor? Thick, smooth rock layers have been building up there for millions of years. Nuclear wastes deposited in these rock layers would probably remain there almost forever.

▲ ▶ **Earthquakes can cause great harm to property and people. But if earthquakes could be predictea, people, at least, might escape unharmed.**

But something "strange" was not happening. In fact, something pretty common was about to happen. And within minutes it did!

The ground moved. Trees swayed in the still air. A frightening rumble echoed through the surrounding hills.

"Earthquake!" cried George.

In the distance, the lights of the great city went out.

"That's home!" the two campers said at the same time as they leaped to their feet.

"We've got to get to a phone quickly." urged George.

The men ran through the woods until they reached a roadside telephone booth. George dialed the emergency police number.

"Park police. Can I help you?"

"Yes," shouted George. "There's been an earthquake. What happened to the city?"

"Calm down, sir," replied a reassuring voice. "Where have you been for the last two weeks?"

"Camping out in the woods," George answered.

"Then you don't know," said the officer. "An earthquake was predicted 10 days ago. Everyone got out of the city safely. Some

buildings are all smashed up, bridges are down, roads are cracked and bent. But no one got hurt."

PREDICTING EARTHQUAKES

What kinds of clues can help scientists predict earthquakes? The events observed by George and his friend signal an earthquake but come too late. There are other events that only scientists using special instruments can observe. Let's take a closer look at some of these events, what may cause them, and how they can be detected.

Throughout history, people have reported seeing a strange glow in the sky moments before an earthquake shakes the land. Scientists explain that the forces that cause an earthquake first squeeze rocks within the Earth with incredible pressure. The rocks often respond by giving off electricity and magnetism. This energy "escapes" into the air, causing the eerie glow. Special electronic instruments can detect changes in the magnetic properties of rocks. Such changes might someday be used to help predict an upcoming earthquake.

Something else seems to happen when rocks deep in the Earth are squeezed under great pressure. The rocks crack and give off a radioactive gas called radon. Some of this gas may enter water in deep wells. Some may escape into the air. In either case, the gas can be detected by instruments that pick up changes in radioactivity. So a sudden increase in the radioactivity of well water or the air may signal a tremor on the way.

What happens when someone squeezes your hand very hard in a handshake? For one thing, your knuckles might crack. Rocks under pressure can do the same thing. Only, unlike the cracking sound knuckles make, the "groans" of rocks are often too low to be heard by the unaided human ear. But specially designed instruments can help scientists listen in on such sounds. The rocks may be trying to tell us something about earthquakes.

Many violent events occur in the Earth when huge sections of rock split apart. Parts of the ground above may tilt or bulge. Other parts may begin to creep past one another. A complex instrument called the tiltmeter can detect changes in the ground's slope as slight as one ten-millionth of a degree, or about half the thickness of this page, over a distance of one kilometer!

Laser beams, which travel at the speed of light, are used to measure creep. A laser beam is fired across a fault, or crack, in the Earth. The beam hits a reflector and bounces back. A special clock times the round trip. If the time of the round trip changes, the distance between the laser "gun" and the reflector has changed. This is a sure sign of creep and a possible warning of greater motions to come.

ANIMAL EARTHQUAKE PREDICTORS

And what about the fish that George and his friend saw leaping out of the nearby lake? How could they, and other animals, help predict earthquakes?

Many animals, such as dogs, can hear sounds that people cannot hear. People have noticed that their pets acted strangely before a quake struck. Changes in the chemical nature of the air are known to affect the brains of rodents such as rats. Scientists have evidence that birds can sense magnetic forces. Sharks are also thought to be sensitive to magnetic forces.

Animals that have these "super senses" might detect and react to changes triggered by a coming earthquake. Scientists are investigating the value of using people to report on strange animal behavior. The scientists have been studying local earthquake data to discover whether animal behavior is related to earthquake activity. Perhaps a pet poodle will one day be used as an earthquake early warning system.

Scientists use special devices to study earthquakes. Seismographs record the strength of an earthquake and how long it lasts (left). Lasers measure how far the land shifts along a fault (right).

For Further Reading

If you have been intrigued by the concepts examined in this textbook, you may also be interested in the ways fellow thinkers—novelists, poets, essayists, as well as scientists—have imaginatively explored the same ideas.

Chapter 1: Movement of the Earth's Crust

Cleaver, Vera. *Where the Lilies Bloom*. Philadelphia, PA: Lippincott.

Hintz, Martin. *Norway*. Chicago, IL: Children's Press.

Ibsen, Henrik. *Peer Gynt*. New York: Airmont.

Lammers, George E. *Time and Life: Fossils Tell the Earth's Story*. New York: Hyperion Press.

Lye, Keith. *Mountains*. Englewood Cliffs, NJ: Silver Burdett.

McPhee, John. *Rising from the Plains*. New York: Farrar, Straus & Giroux.

Chapter 2: Earthquakes and Volcanoes

Daggett, R.M. *The Legends and Myths of Hawaii: The Fables and Folk-lore of a Strange People*. Rutland, VT: C.E. Tuttle.

Gilbreath, Alice. *Ring of Fire: And the Hawaiian Islands and Iceland*. Minneapolis, MN: Dillon.

Hills, C.A.R. *A Day that Made History: The Destruction of Pompeii and Herculaneum*. London, England: Dryad Press.

House, James. *The San Francisco Earthquake*. San Diego, CA: Lucent Books.

Nardo, Don. *Krakatoa*. San Diego, CA: Lucent Books.

Chapter 3: Plate Tectonics

Corbalis, Judy. *The Ice-Cream Heroes*. Boston, MA: Little, Brown.

Lampton, Christopher. *Mass Extinctions: One Theory of Why the Dinosaurs Vanished*. New York: Watts.

Miller, Russell. *Continents in Collision*. Alexandria, VA: Time-Life.

Spyri, Johanna. *Heidi*. Teaneck, NJ: Sharon Publications.

Ullman, James Ramsey. *Banner in the Sky*. Philadelphia, PA: Lippincott.

Chapter 4: Rocks and Minerals

Llewellyn, Richard. *How Green Was My Valley*. New York: Dell.

Martin, John H. *A Day in the Life of a High-Iron Worker*. Mahwah, NJ: Troll.

Pope, Elizabeth Marie. *The Sherwood Ring*. Boston, MA: Houghton Mifflin.

Pullman, Philip. *The Ruby in the Smoke*. New York: Knopf.

Roop, Peter, and Connie Roop. *Stonehenge: Opposing Viewpoints*. San Diego, CA: Greenhaven.

Chapter 5: Weathering and Soil Formation

Bacon, Katherine J. *Shadow and Light*. New York: Macmillan.

Cleaver, Vera, and Bill Cleaver. *Dust of the Earth*. New York: Harper & Row Junior Books.

St. George, Judith. *The Mount Rushmore Story*. New York: Putnam.

Steinbeck, John. *The Grapes of Wrath*. New York: Viking.

Thackeray, Sue. *Looking at Pollution*. London, England: Trafalgar Square.

Chapter 6: Erosion and Deposition

Bramwell, Martyn. *Glaciers and Ice Caps*. New York: Watts.

Buck, Pearl S. *The Good Earth*. New York: T.Y. Crowell.

Clark, Walter V. *The Ox-Bow Incident*. New York: New American Library.

Smith, Don. *The Grand Canyon: Journey Through Time*. Mahwah, NJ: Troll.

Steele, David H. *The Pebble Searcher*. London, England: A.H. Stockwell.

Wibberly, Leonard. *Attar of the Ice Valley*. New York: Farrar, Straus & Giroux.

The metric system of measurement is used by scientists throughout the world. It is based on units of ten. Each unit is ten times larger or ten times smaller than the next unit. The most commonly used units of the metric system are given below. After you have finished reading about the metric system, try to put it to use. How tall are you in metrics? What is your mass? What is your normal body temperature in degrees Celsius?

Commonly Used Metric Units

Length
Length The distance from one point to another

meter (m)   A meter is slightly longer than a yard.
1 meter = 1000 millimeters (mm)
1 meter = 100 centimeters (cm)
1000 meters = 1 kilometer (km)

Volume
Volume The amount of space an object takes up

liter (L)   A liter is slightly more than a quart.
1 liter = 1000 milliliters (mL)

Mass
Mass The amount of matter in an object

gram (g)   A gram has a mass equal to about one paper clip.

1000 grams = 1 kilogram (kg)

Temperature
Temperature The measure of hotness or coldness

degrees   0°C = freezing point of water
Celsius (°C)   100°C = boiling point of water

Metric–English Equivalents

2.54 centimeters (cm) = 1 inch (in.)
1 meter (m) = 39.37 inches (in.)
1 kilometer (km) = 0.62 miles (mi)
1 liter (L) = 1.06 quarts (qt)
250 milliliters (mL) = 1 cup (c)
1 kilogram (kg) = 2.2 pounds (lb)
28.3 grams (g) = 1 ounce (oz)
°C = 5/9 × (°F − 32)

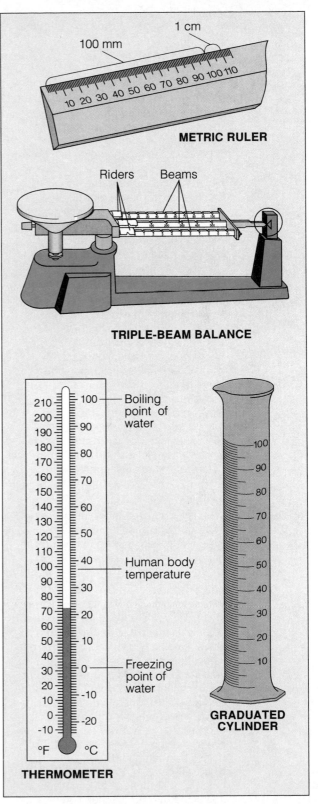

METRIC RULER

TRIPLE-BEAM BALANCE

THERMOMETER

GRADUATED CYLINDER

Glassware Safety

1. Whenever you see this symbol, you will know that you are working with glassware that can easily be broken. Take particular care to handle such glassware safely. And never use broken or chipped glassware.
2. Never heat glassware that is not thoroughly dry. Never pick up any glassware unless you are sure it is not hot. If it is hot, use heat-resistant gloves.
3. Always clean glassware thoroughly before putting it away.

Fire Safety

1. Whenever you see this symbol, you will know that you are working with fire. Never use any source of fire without wearing safety goggles.
2. Never heat anything—particularly chemicals—unless instructed to do so.
3. Never heat anything in a closed container.
4. Never reach across a flame.
5. Always use a clamp, tongs, or heat-resistant gloves to handle hot objects.
6. Always maintain a clean work area, particularly when using a flame.

Heat Safety

Whenever you see this symbol, you will know that you should put on heat-resistant gloves to avoid burning your hands.

Chemical Safety

1. Whenever you see this symbol, you will know that you are working with chemicals that could be hazardous.
2. Never smell any chemical directly from its container. Always use your hand to waft some of the odors from the top of the container toward your nose—and only when instructed to do so.
3. Never mix chemicals unless instructed to do so.
4. Never touch or taste any chemical unless instructed to do so.
5. Keep all lids closed when chemicals are not in use. Dispose of all chemicals as instructed by your teacher.

6. Immediately rinse with water any chemicals, particularly acids, that get on your skin and clothes. Then notify your teacher.

Eye and Face Safety

1. Whenever you see this symbol, you will know that you are performing an experiment in which you must take precautions to protect your eyes and face by wearing safety goggles.
2. When you are heating a test tube or bottle, always point it away from you and others. Chemicals can splash or boil out of a heated test tube.

Sharp Instrument Safety

1. Whenever you see this symbol, you will know that you are working with a sharp instrument.
2. Always use single-edged razors; double-edged razors are too dangerous.
3. Handle any sharp instrument with extreme care. Never cut any material toward you; always cut away from you.
4. Immediately notify your teacher if your skin is cut.

Electrical Safety

1. Whenever you see this symbol, you will know that you are using electricity in the laboratory.
2. Never use long extension cords to plug in any electrical device. Do not plug too many appliances into one socket or you may overload the socket and cause a fire.
3. Never touch an electrical appliance or outlet with wet hands.

Animal Safety

1. Whenever you see this symbol, you will know that you are working with live animals.
2. Do not cause pain, discomfort, or injury to an animal.
3. Follow your teacher's directions when handling animals. Wash your hands thoroughly after handling animals or their cages.

Glossary

abrasion (uh-BRAY-zhuhn): the wearing away of a substance by solid particles carried by wind, water, or other forces

alluvial fan: a fan-shaped deposit of sediments formed at the point where a river leaves the mountains and runs out onto a plain

anticline (AN-tih-klighn): an upward fold in rock

bedrock: the layer of rock beneath the soil

caldera: a roughly circular, steep-sided pit at the top of a volcanic cone whose diameter is at least three times its depth

carbonation: the process in which carbonic acid reacts chemically with other substances

chemical rock: a non-clastic sedimentary rock formed by inorganic processes such as evaporation

chemical weathering: weathering that involves changes in the chemical makeup of rocks

cinder cone: a volcano made mostly of cinders and other rock particles that have been blown into the air

cinder: a small, rough volcanic bomb no more than several centimeters across

clastic rock: a sedimentary rock formed from fragments of previously existing rocks

cleavage: the tendency of a mineral to break along smooth, definite surfaces

composite volcano: a volcano built of alternating layers of rock particles and lava

compression: the type of stress that squeezes rocks together

convection current: a movement of material caused by differences in temperature

convergent (kuhn-VER-jehnt) **boundary:** a plate boundary at which plates come together

crater: a funnel-shaped pit at the top of a volcanic cone whose diameter is less than three times its depth

crust: the surface layer of the Earth

crystal: a solid in which the atoms or molecules are arranged in a definite pattern that is repeated over and over again

deformation: in geology, any change in the original shape or volume of rocks

delta: a triangular formation of sediments deposited at the mouth of a large river that flows into a lake or ocean

density: the amount of matter in a given space; the mass per unit volume

deposition (dehp-uh-ZIHSH-uhn): the process by which sediments are laid down in new locations

divergent (digh-VER-jehnt) **boundary:** a plate boundary at which plates move apart

dome: a raised area shaped roughly like the top half of a sphere, often formed by magma pushing upward on the rock layers above it

drainage basin: the area drained by a main river and its channels

drainage system: the network of streams and other bodies of running water that ultimately drain into an area's main river

drumlin: an oval-shaped mound of till

earthquake: the shaking and trembling that results from the sudden movement of part of the Earth's crust

epicenter (EHP-uh-sehn-tuhr): the point on the Earth's surface directly above the focus of an earthquake

erosion (ee-ROH-zhuhn): the process by which the products of weathering are moved from one place to another

exfoliation (ehks-foh-lee-AY-shuhn): the breaking off of curved sheets or slabs parallel to a rock's surface due to weathering

extrusive (ehk-STROO-sihv) **rock:** an igneous rock formed from lava

fault-block mountain: a mountain formed by blocks of rock uplifted from normal faults

fault: a break or crack along which rocks move

flood plain: a flat area that is found on both sides of a river or stream and is formed by sediments deposited during floods

focus (FOH-cuhs): the underground point of origin of an earthquake, where the rocks break and move

fold: a bend in rock

foot wall: the block of rock below a fault

fossil: the preserved remains or traces of an ancient organism

fracture: break or crack

fracture: in minerals, the way a mineral that does not cleave breaks along a rough or jagged surface

frost action: the breaking apart of a rock caused by the water freezing and expanding within cracks

gemstone: a hard, beautiful, durable substance that can be cut and polished for jewelry and decoration

glacier (GLAY-shuhr): a large mass of moving ice and snow

hanging wall: the block of rock above a fault

hardness: the ability of a mineral to resist being scratched

horizon (huh-RIGH-zuhn): soil layer

humus (HYOO-muhs): the part of the soil formed by decaying organic material

iceberg: a part of a glacier that has broken off and drifted into the sea

igneous (IHG-nee-uhs): formed from molten rock

immature river: a river in an early stage of development

inorganic: not formed from living things or the remains of living things

intrusive (ihn-TROO-sihv) **rock:** an igneous rock formed from magma

isostasy (igh-SAHS-tuh-see): the balancing of the downward force of the crust and the upward force of the mantle

kettle lake: a round, deep lake formed by a huge block of ice left behind by a glacier

landslide: a large downhill movement of loose rocks and soil caused by the pull of gravity

lateral fault: a fault along which the blocks move horizontally past each other

lava: molten rock at the Earth's surface

leaching (LEECH-ihng): the process in which water washes minerals from the topsoil to the subsoil

levee (LEHV-ee): in nature, a ridgelike deposit along the sides of a river

lithosphere (LIHTH-oh-sfeer): the topmost solid part of the Earth, which is composed of the crust and some of the mantle

load: the amount of sediment carried by a stream

loess (LOH-ehs): accumulations of fine particles of sand and silt deposited by the wind

longshore current: the movement of water parallel to a shoreline

luster: the way a mineral reflects light from its surface

magma: molten rock beneath the Earth's surface

mantle: the layer of the Earth that extends from the bottom of the crust to the core

mass wasting: the downhill movement of sediments due to gravity

mature river: a river that has been developing for many thousands of years

meander (mee-AN-der): a loop in a river

mechanical weathering: weathering that does not involve changes in the chemical makeup of rocks

meltwater: formed by the water from melting ice or snow; water from melting ice or snow

metal: an element that is shiny, conducts electricity and heat, and is easily shaped

metamorphic (meht-ah-MOR-fihk): changed in form as a result of chemical reactions, heat, and/or pressure

metamorphism (meht-ah-MOR-fihz-uhm): the process in which metamorphic rock is formed

midocean ridge: an undersea mountain chain where new ocean floor is produced; a constructive (divergent) plate boundary

mineral: a naturally occurring, inorganic solid that has a definite chemical composition and crystal shape

moraine: a ridge of till left behind by a retreating glacier

nonmetal: an element that has a dull surface, is a poor conductor of electricity and heat, and is not easily shaped

normal fault: a fault in which the hanging wall moves down relative to the foot wall

ocean-floor spreading: the process in which old ocean floor is pushed away from a midocean ridge by the formation of new ocean floor

ore: a mineral or rock from which metals and nonmetals can be removed in usable amounts

organic rock: a sedimentary rock that is formed either directly or indirectly from material that was once alive

outwash plain: flat, fan-shaped areas in front of terminal moraines formed by sediments deposited by rivers of glacial meltwater

oxbow lake: a U-shaped lake formed when erosion and deposition cuts off a meander of a river

oxidation (ahk-suh-DAY-shuhn): the process in which oxygen chemically combines with another substance

Pangaea (pan-JEE-ah): the single giant landmass that existed more than 200 million years ago and that gave rise to the present-day continents

plate: in plate tectonics, one of the moving, irregularly shaped slabs that make up the Earth's lithosphere

plateau (pla-TOH): a large area of flat land that is raised high above sea level and that consists of horizontal rock layers

pore space: a space between soil particles

primary wave, P wave: a push-pull seismic wave, which can travel through solids, liquids, and gases; P waves are the fastest type of seismic wave

residual (rih-ZIHJ-oo-uhl) **soil:** soil that remains on top of the rock from which it was formed

reverse fault: a fault in which the hanging wall moves up relative to the foot wall

Richter scale: the scale used to measure the strength of earthquakes

rift valley: a valley formed when the block of land between two normal faults slides downward

Ring of Fire: the earthquake and volcano zone that encircles the Pacific Ocean

rock cycle: the interrelated processes that cause the continuous changing of rocks from one kind to another

rock: a hard substance composed of one or more minerals or minerallike substances

root-pry: the breaking apart of rocks caused by the growth of plant roots

sand bar: a long, underwater ridge of sand

sand dune: a mound of sand deposited by the wind

sea cave: a hollowed out portion of a sea cliff

sea cliff: a steep face of rock produced by wave action

sea stack: a column of resistant rock left behind after a sea cliff has been eroded away

secondary wave, S wave: a side-to-side earthquake wave, which can travel through solids but not through liquids and gases; S waves are slower than P waves but faster than L waves

sediment (SEHD-ih-mehnt): particles of rock or organic materials that have been carried along and deposited by water and/or wind

sedimentary (sehd-ih-MEHN-tuh-ree): formed by the compacting and cementing of sediments or by other non-igneous processes at the Earth's surface

seismic (SIGHZ-mihk) **wave:** an earthquake wave

seismogram (SIGHZ-muh-gram): a record of seismic waves recorded by a seismograph

seismograph (SIGHZ-muh-grahf): an instrument that detects and measures seismic waves

seismologist (sighz-MUHL-oh-jihst): a scientist who studies earthquakes

shearing: the type of stress that pushes rocks of the crust in two opposite, horizontal directions

shield volcano: a volcano composed of quiet lava flows

soil profile: a cross section of soil horizons

spit: a sandbar connected to the shoreline

stable rock: a rock composed of minerals that resist chemical weathering

streak: the color of the powder left by a mineral when it is rubbed against a hard, rough surface

stress: the forces that push and pull on the Earth's crust, causing its deformation

strike-slip boundary: a plate boundary at which two plates slip past one another horizontally

subduction (suhb-DUHK-shuhn): the process in which crust plunges back into the interior of the Earth

subsoil: the soil in the B horizon, or middle layer of soil

surface wave, L wave: a up-and-down earthquake wave; L waves are the slowest-moving seismic waves

syncline (SIHN-klighn): a downward fold in rock

tectonics (tehk-TAHN-ihks): the branch of geology that deals with the movements that shape the Earth's crust

tension: the type of stress that pulls rocks apart

terrace: a flat platform of rocks, sand, and silt at the base of a sea cliff

theory of continental drift: the theory, proposed by Alfred Wegener, that the continents were once joined together and have since drifted apart

theory of plate tectonics: the theory that links together the ideas of continental drift and ocean-floor spreading and explains how the Earth has changed over time

thrust fault: a reverse fault in which the hanging wall slides over the foot wall

till: the rocks and debris deposited directly by a glacier

topsoil: the soil in the A horizon, or uppermost layer of mature soil

transform fault: a fault that runs across a midocean ridge

transported soil: soil that is moved away from its place of origin

trench: a V-shaped valley on the ocean floor where old ocean floor is subducted; a destructive (convergent) plate boundary

tributary (TRIHB-yoo-tehr-ee): a large stream or small river that flows into an area's main river

tsunami (tsoo-NAH-mee): a giant sea wave produced by an earthquake

vent: an opening through which lava erupts

volcanic ash: rock particles more than 0.25 mm but less than 5 mm across that are blown into the air by a volcanic eruption

volcanic bomb: rock particles larger than 5 mm in diameter that are blown into the air by a volcanic eruption

volcanic dust: the smallest rock particles blown into the air by a volcanic eruption

volcano: a place in the Earth's surface through which molten rock and other materials reach the surface

weathering: the breaking down of rocks and other materials at the Earth's surface

Index

Gypsum, J86, J103

Halite, J87, J89
Hanging wall, J15
Hardness, J84–85
    Field hardness scale, J85
    Mohs scale, J84–85
Hawaii, formation of, J42
Hematite, J85, J89
Herculaneum, J49
Himalayan Mountains, J69
Hope diamond, J79
Horizons, soil, J124–125

Ice Age, J147
Icebergs, J148–149
Iceland, formation of, J42
Igneous rocks, J93–94, J97–100
    composition, J97
    extrusive rocks, J99
    intrusive rocks, J99
    textures, J98–99
Immature river, J143
Indonesia, J69
Inorganic substance, J80
Intrusive rocks, J99
Iron, J88, J89
Iron oxide, J118
Island arcs, J69
Isostasy, J22–23

Japan, J69
Joints, and fractures of rocks, J14

Kettle lakes, J150

Lakes
    glacial lakes, J149–150
    kettle lakes, J150
Landslides, J135
    and mechanical weathering, J116
Lassen Peak, J46
Lateral fault, J16
Lateral moraine, J147
Lava, J20, J40–41
    types of, J41–42
Leaching, soil, J125
Lead, J88, J89
Levee, J145
Lewis Overthrust Fault, J15
Limestone
    as chemical rock, J103–104
    as organic rock, J101–102
Limonite, J89
Lithosphere, J65
Lithospheric plates, J65–66
Load, streams, 141
Loess, J138–139
    formation of, J138
    locations of, J138–139
    and windbreaks, J139
Longshore currents, J153

Luster of minerals, J84

Magma, J20, J40, J99
Magnetic poles, reversal of, J62
Magnetite, J87
Malachite, J83
Mantle, J22–23, J63, J65, J65
Marble, J107
Mass wasting, J135–136
    earthflows, J136
    landslides, J135
    mudflows, J135
    slump, J135
    soil creep, J136
Mature river, J143
Mauna Loa, J44
Meanders, rivers, J143
Mechanical weathering, J115–117
Mediterranean Zone, J48
Meltwater deposits, J148
Metals, J88–89
    uses of, J89
Metamorphic rocks, J94
    classification of, J106–107
    formation of, J105–106
    types of, J106
Metamorphism, J105, J106
Mid-Atlantic Ridge, J48
Midocean ridges, J60–61, J66
    transform faults, J61
Milne, John, J36
Minerals
    cleavage, J86–87
    color of, J83
    crystal shape, J86
    definition of, J80
    density, J86
    formation of, J81–82
    fracture, J86–87
    gemstones, J90
    hardness, J84–85
    luster, J84
    rock-forming minerals, J82
    special properties of, J87
    streak, J85–86
Mining, metals, J88–89
Mississippi River, J24, J145
Mississippi River Valley, J138
Mohs, Friedrich, J84
Molten rock, J20, J40, J69
Moraines, J147, J148
Mountains
    dome mountains, J20
    fault-block mountains, J16
    folded chains, J17
Mount Etna, J45
Mount Hood, J46
Mount Katmai, J46
Mount Pinatubo, J31
Mount Ranier, J46
Mount Rushmore, J113
Mount St. Helens, J46
Mount Shasta, J46

Mount Vesuvius, J45, J49
Mudflows, J135

Nile River, flooding of, J155
Nonmetals, J89
Normal fault, J15

Obsidian, J98, J99
Ocean-floor spreading, J60–63
Oceanic crust, J12
Ores, J88–89
    smelting, J89–90
Organic rock, J102–103
Outwash plains, J148
Oxbow lakes, J144
Oxidation, and chemical
    weathering, J117–118

Pangaea, J56–57
Paricutín, J44
Pegmatite, J99
Plant acids, and chemical
    weathering, J118
Plate boundaries, J66–67
    convergent boundaries, J66
    divergent boundaries, J66
    strike-slip boundaries, J67
Plate motion
    and convection currents, J67–68
    plate collisions, J68–71
Plate tectonics
    continental drift, J56–59
    and evolution of living things,
        J73
    lithospheric plates, J65–66
    ocean-floor spreading, J60–63
    plate boundaries, J66–67
    plate motion, J67–71
    theory of, J64, J71
Plateaus, J18–20
Plutonic rocks, J99
Pompeii, J49
Pore spaces, soil, J123
Porphyritic rocks, J98
Precious stones, J90
Puddingstones, J101
Pumice, J42, J99
Pyrite, J84

Quartz, J83, J84, J86, J95, J97
Quartzite, J87, J107

Reefs, J103
Reverse fault, J15
Rhyolite, J42
Richter, Charles, J37
Richter scale, J37–38
Rills, J140, J142
Ring of Fire, J47, J66
Rivers, J142–145
    alluvial fans, J144
    deltas, J144–145

CREDITS

Cover Background: Ken Karp
Photo Research: Omni-Photo Communications, Inc.
Contributing Artists: Illustrations: Warren Budd Assoc. Ltd., Gerry Schrenk, Mark Schuller. Charts and graphs: Function Thru Form
Photographs: 5 Dr. E. R. Degginger; 6 top: Lefever/Grushow/ Grant Heilman Photography; center: Index Stock Photography, Inc.; bottom: Rex Joseph; 8 top: James Blank/Stock Market; bottom: Soames Summerhays/ Science Source/ Photo Researchers, Inc.; 9 Douglas Faulkner/Photo Researchers, Inc.; 10 and 11 Jeff Gnass Photography; 12 left: Kent & Donna Dannen/Photo Researchers, Inc.; right: David Muench Photography Inc.; 13 G. R. Roberts/Omni-Photo Communications, Inc.; 14 left: G. R. Roberts/Omni-Photo Communications, Inc.; right: Geoff Johnson/Tony Stone Worldwide/ Chicago Ltd.; 15 Steve Kaufman/Peter Arnold, Inc.; right: Robert P. Comport/Animals Animals/Earth Scenes; 17 top: Dr. Nigel Smith/Animals Animals/Earth Scenes; bottom: G. R. Roberts/Omni-Photo Communications, Inc.; 19 left: Douglas Faulkner/Photo Researchers, Inc.; right: Victor Englebert/Photo Researchers, Inc.; 20 Doug Wechsler/Animals Animals/Earth Scenes; 21 Kent & Donna Dannen/Photo Researchers, Inc.; 22 Elaine Braithwaite/ Peter Arnold, Inc.; 25 left: Werner H. Müller/Peter Arnold, Inc.; right: M. Long/ Envision; 29 Carl Frank/ Photo Researchers, Inc.; 30 and 31 Alon Reininger/ Contact Press Images/ Woodfin Camp & Associates; 32 Frank Fournier/Contact Press Images/Woodfin Camp & Associates; 33 top: William Felger/Grant Heilman Photography; bottom: Jules Bucher/ Photo Researchers, Inc.; 36 Clarence R. Allen/Seismological Laboratory/California Institute of Technology; 37 left and right: Granger Collection; 38 West Light; 41 top: Reuters/Bettmann; bottom: US Geological Survey; 42 top and bottom: William E. Ferguson; 43 top to bottom: Gary Rosenquist/Earth Images; 44 top: Reuters/Bettmann; bottom: J. C. Ratte/ USGS; 45 left: Jerry Frank/DPI; center: Thomas Nebbia/Woodfin Camp & Associates; right: G. R. Roberts/Omni-Photo Communications, Inc.; 46 left: Mike Severns/Tom Stack & Associates; right: Joe McDonald/Animals Animals/Earth Scenes; 49 left and right: Scala/Art Resource; center: Napoli, Museo Nazionale/Scala/Art Resource; 53 Granger Collection; 54 and 55 USGS/EROS; 57 Martin Land/Science Photo Library/Photo Researchers, Inc.; 58 Bob Abraham/Stock Market; 59 Kunio Owaki/Stock Market; 60 left: John Shelton; right: Ragnar Larusson/Photo Researchers, Inc.; 63 Robert D. Ballard/ Woods Hole Oceanographic Institution; 66 Marie Tharp, Rebecca M. Espinosa; 67 David Parker/Science Photo Library/Photo Researchers, Inc.; 69 Catherine Ursillo/Photo Researchers, Inc.; 73 top: Tom McHugh/Photo Researchers, Inc.; center: Esao Hashimoto/Animals Animals/Earth Scenes; bottom: Tom McHugh/Photo Researchers, Inc.; 78 and 79 Fred Ward/ Black Star; 80 top: Dr. E. R. Degginger; center: Breck P. Kent; bottom: Stephenie S. Ferguson; 81 left and top right: William E. Ferguson; bottom right: Manfred Kage/ Peter Arnold, Inc.; 82 left: Carl Frank/Photo Researchers, Inc.; right: Martin Land/ Science Photo Library/Photo Researchers, Inc.; 83 top left: J. Cancalosi/Peter Arnold, Inc.; top center and bottom right: Dr. E. R. Degginger; top right: Martin Land/ Science Photo Library/Photo Research ers, Inc.; bottom left: Paul Silverman/Fundamental Photographs; bottom center: Dennis Purse/Photo Researchers, Inc.; 84 top left: Manfred Kage/ Peter Arnold, Inc.; center and right: Dr. E. R. Degginger; bottom left: J & L Weber/Peter Arnold, Inc.; 86 far left, center right, and far right: Dr. E. R. Degginger; left: Robert De Gugliemo/Science Photo Library/Photo Researchers, Inc.; center left: Roberto De Gugliemo/ Photo Researchers, Inc.; right: Jeffrey Scovil; 87 top left, top center, and top right: Grace Davies/Omni-Photo Communications, Inc.; center right and bottom right: Dr. E. R. Degginger; 88 left: Ken Karp/Omni-Photo Communications, Inc.; right: Dr. E. R. Degginger; 89 left and right: Dr. E. R. Degginger; 90 top left, center, and right: Photograph by Erica and Harold Van Pelt, courtesy American Museum of Natural History; bottom left: Steve Vidler/Leo De Wys, Inc.; 92 top right, bottom left, and bottom right: Fred Ward/Black Star; center right: GE Corporation; 93 Nicole Galeazzi/Omni-Photo Communications, Inc.; 94 left: Soames Summerhays/Photo Researchers, Inc.; center and right: Breck P. Kent; 95 top: Spencer Swanger/Tom Stack & Associates; bottom left and bottom right: Dr. E. R. Degginger; 96 top left, top right, bottom left, and bottom right: Dr. E. R. Degginger; 98 top left and bottom right: Dr. E. R. Degginger; top right: Joyce Photographics/ Photo Researchers, Inc.; bottom left: Breck P. Kent; 99 left and right: Breck P. Kent; 100 Dr. E. R. Degginger; 101 left: Gerald Corsi/Tom Stack & Associates; top right: Breck P. Kent; center right: John Buitenkant/Photo Researchers, Inc.; bottom right: Dr. E. R. Degginger; 102 top left: Dr. E. R. Degginger; bottom left: G. R. Roberts/Omni-Photo Communications, Inc.; right: Stephenie S. Ferguson; 103 left: Phil Degginger; right: Bjorn Bolstad/Peter Arnold, Inc.; 104 top left: Don Carroll/Image Bank; top right: John Cancalosi/Peter Arnold, Inc.; center left: John S. Shelton; bottom left: G. R. Roberts/Omni-Photo Communications, Inc.; bottom right: Bob McKeever/Tom Stack & Associates; 105 left: Breck P. Kent; right: D. Cavagnaro/Peter Arnold, Inc.; 106 top and center top: Hubbard Scientific; center bottom and bottom: Breck P. Kent; 107 Breck P. Kent; 111 Photograph by Erica and Harold Van Pelt, courtesy American Museum of Natural History; 112 and 113 National Park Service; 114 left: William E. Ferguson; right: John Mead/ Science Photo Library/Photo Researchers, Inc.; 115 B. G. Murray, Jr./Animals Animals/Earth Scenes; 116 top and bottom: William E. Ferguson; bottom left: Henryk Tomasz Kaiser/Envision; 117 left: William E. Ferguson; right: Charlie Ott/Photo Researchers, Inc.; 118 Robert Lee/Photo Researchers, Inc.; 119 left: Adrienne T. Gibson/Animals Animals/ Earth Scenes; right: John S. Shelton; 120 left: Fred Whitehead/Animals Animals/Earth Scenes; right: Ilona Backhaus/Okapia/ Photo Researchers, Inc.; 123 top and bottom: USDA; 124 top: Walter Dawn; bottom: USDA; 125 Brian Parker/Tom Stack & Associates; 126 left: Dr. E. R. Degginger; right: Omni-Photo Communications, Inc.; 127 top: Asa C. Thoresen/Photo Researchers, Inc.; bottom: Chip & Jill Isenhart/Tom Stack & Associates; 132 and 133: Chester Christian/Alpha; 134 R. Valentine Atkinson/Focus on Sports; 135 left: William E. Ferguson; center: Tom McHugh/Photo Researchers, Inc.; right: G. R. Roberts/Omni-Photo Communications, Inc.; 137 left: Tony Stone Worldwide/ Chicago Ltd.; right: Galen Rowell/ Peter Arnold, Inc.; 138 top left: Terry Donnelly/Tom Stack & Associates; top right: Ken Biggs/Tony Stone Worldwide/Chicago Ltd.; bottom: G. R. Roberts/Omni-Photo Communications, Inc.; 141 William E. Ferguson; 142 top: Lenore Weber/Omni-Photo Communications, Inc.; bottom: NASA/Omni-Photo Communications, Inc.; 143 left: Garry D. McMichael/Photo Researchers, Inc.; right: Pat and Tom Leeson/Photo Researchers, Inc.; 144 G. R. Roberts/Omni-Photo Communications, Inc.; 145 left: G. R. Roberts/Omni-Photo Communications, Inc.; right: Andrew Rakoczy/Photo Researchers, Inc.; 146 left: Stephen J. Krasemann/Peter Arnold, Inc.; right: Roger Mear/Tony Stone Worldwide/Chicago Ltd.; 147 top: Omni-Photo Communications, Inc.; bottom: NASA; 148 top: Helmut Gritscher/Peter Arnold, Inc.; bottom: Dr. E. R. Degginger; 149 left: Frans Lanting/Minden Pictures, Inc.; right: Stephenie S. Ferguson; 151 left: William E. Ferguson; right: Ed Cooper; 152 left: Suzanne and Nick Geary/Tony Stone Worldwide/Chicago Ltd.; right: Dr. E. R. Degginger; 153 top: Lawrence Manning/Tony Stone Worldwide/Chicago Ltd.; bottom left: Peter Newton/Tony Stone Worldwide/Chicago Ltd.; bottom right: C. Seghers/Photo Researchers, Inc.; 155 left: E.R.I.M./Tony Stone Worldwide/Chicago Ltd.; right: Farrell Grehan/Photo Researchers, Inc.; 159 Martin Wendler/Peter Arnold, Inc.; 160 top: Giraudon/Art Resource; bottom: Joe McNally/© 1984 Discover Magazine; 161 Joe McNally/© 1984 Discover Magazine; 162 Mike J. Howell/Envision; 163 and 164 Department of Energy; 166 left: David J. Cross/Peter Arnold, Inc.; right: UPI/Bettmann; 167 left: Michael Salas/Image Bank; right: Chuck O'Rear/Woodfin Camp & Associates; 168 David Muench Photography Inc.; 174 Victor Englebert/Photo Researchers, Inc.